DEDICATION

This book is dedicated to those persons, like myself, who have been scared almost witless when they have encountered a phenomenon they could not understand.

A shadow world does exist, a world out of the corner of the eye. Most of us have experienced a feeling that we were being silently observed by an unseen something. We have heard faint, indistinct sounds which we could not identify, or perhaps seen a fleeting, unexplainable shadow as if something from the unknown had approached our edge of reality, trying in some manner to communicate with us. We have been gripped by an eerie, mysterious, intangible feeling that for no logical reason causes us to momentarily shiver.

It is to those persons who have experienced such emotions that I leave this work to ponder.

ACKNOWLEDGEMENTS

No one who writes a book based on historical events or local legend does so alone. The help of others is essential to the successful completion of such an undertaking. For their valuable assistance in gathering information for these stories, I am deeply indebted to many people.

To maintain anonymity for those individuals and families who might prefer to remain unidentified, I have changed the names of people and places involved in these stories. The incidents, however, are based on information relayed to me as factual. Indeed, the people involved in specific happenings, including me, were convinced that the events were real...that they have actually seen, felt or heard these unexplainable revealments.

Tragedy at Devil's Hollow
and other Kentucky Ghost Stories

Michael Paul Henson

The Overmountain Press

JOHNSON CITY, TENNESSEE

ISBN: 1-57072-160-2

1 2 3 4 5 6 7 8 9 0

TABLE OF CONTENTS

PART I — Ghost Stories

PART II — Unexplained Phenomena

PREFACE

"Proof is being shown every day
that there is more realism in folklore than we experience in our dreams."

All too often authentic folklore has been caught up in the backwash of time. Nearly forgotten, it has disappeared into the pages of neglected histories or been all but lost in the retelling of legends. In Kentucky a few ancient ones still remain who know firsthand some of the stories, legends and folklore of our state. With their passing we stand to lose even more of this wonderful heritage.

It is time...time that someone undertakes to collect, at least in part, the scattered remnants and compile them for the present and future generations of Kentuckians. Such is my purpose in this endeavor.

Some of these narratives were related to me by reputable individuals, while still others were found in old newspapers, history books, diaries and other personal documents. Some are drawn from my own experiences.

An author cannot hope to completely cover a subject of this scope and nature. Many strange and unusual stories will forever remain unknown because those familiar with such incidents have chosen to keep them secret for personal reasons, avoiding any possible derision to individuals or families involved.

Particular care has been taken to omit obvious misconceptions from these accounts, but we would remind our readers that there is always room for human error in things that concern the supernatural or unexplained.

Michael Paul Henson

INTRODUCTION

Ghost stories and unexplained phenomena are shrouded in mystery. Their very nature removes them from the field of exact science and the necessity for positive proof. Therefore one view is just as valid as another. One aspect is certain, however...there are more mysteries than known facts, and there will forever be puzzlements to provoke our minds.

Belief in the supernatural is closely akin to belief in religion. Both involve an intensely personal relationship with a preternatural being or design. Thus it should naturally follow that a person with a personal belief in and respect for religion should also possess a tolerant, understanding attitude toward those who believe they have personally encountered a ghost, witch, other supernatural being or unexplained phenomenon. After all, who among us is qualified to sit in judgment of such convictions?

This book is divided into two distinct categories, based upon types of stories and information.

Ghost Stories...These are stories related by individuals who firmly believe they have encountered, through feeling, sight or sound, the disembodied spirit of a deceased person or animal which by some means unknown has materialized or otherwise made itself manifest.

Unexplained Phenomena...These stories differ from Ghost Stories to the extent that they are concerned with unusual facts or occurrences that are directly perceptible, such as odd places, strange happenings, or dreams and visions that came true...things that simply should not exist or should never have occurred.

This is by no means a complete collection of Kentucky folklore. It is a limited selection of ghost stories and unexplained phenomena which is only a small part of that large Kentucky storytelling tradition. The stories contained in this collection are relatively unknown for two principal reasons—first, no one has previously taken the time to collect and compile them; second, these are stories generally limited to certain localities and have seldom been told outside the area of occurrence.

In some instances the basic facts have been obscured by the lapse of time, exaggerated traditions, garbled accounts and the nature of the subject. While some of the stories may have been transmuted through the years of telling, the essence remains the same and the fascination...the intrigue provoked by these tales of wonderment...has not been diminished one whit.

PART I
Ghost Stories

Enchanted Tree

There is an unusual beech tree in western Kentucky... unusual in that it is alive but no leaves will grow from its branches. Legend has it that the tree is enchanted because three innocent young men were hanged from its limbs. This story has never before appeared in print and only a very few people have ever heard it told.

In 1899, a time when most of Kentucky's notorious bad-men were either dead or locked away for life, there were still a few outlaws hiding out among the canebrakes along the Ohio River in western Kentucky. Two among them were the brothers Sam and Levi Jackson. For years, their gang had robbed, stolen, counterfeited and otherwise perpetrated about every evil deed imaginable.

Following one of their nefarious deeds, the Jacksons would usually head for the river. Here they would either hide out in the canebrakes or take a boat downriver. They would lie low until things quieted down, then they would return to their old haunts. Finally, their activities reached such outrageous proportions that local citizens formed a vigilante group in an effort to rid the neighborhood of the scoundrels.

A family living on a small farm across the Ohio River in Illinois was destined for a principal role in the unfortunate drama that was soon to follow. The three young men were on the river bank fishing when Sam, Levi and several other members of this gang came downriver. Spotting the young fishermen, the Jacksons put their boats into shore where they took the youngsters prisoner. Sam, the ring-leader, had planned to rob a nearby bank, and he reasoned that he could lay the blame on the three innocent boys.

At gunpoint, the outlaws forced the teenagers to drink

whiskey until they were barely able to sit on a horse. All three young men were placed on horses which the gang had waiting. The gang members then mounted their horses, surrounded the young men and herded them toward the rendezvous point outside the town where the robbery was to be committed.

When the band arrived at the appointed place, Sam ordered one of his henchmen to stay behind with the boys while the rest went on to town. The plan was for the outlaws to return after the bank robbery, put some of the stolen money on one of the boys, whip the youngsters' horses into a run in one direction while the gang escaped in a different direction. The idea was that the vigilantes would chase the young men instead of the real villains.

Under most circumstances such a plan would not have worked. The vigilantes would have realized that the young men were too drunk to have successfully robbed a bank. Again, fate stepped in. The robbery had taken longer than the outlaws had expected, and the boys were beginning to sober up by the time the robbers returned. During the robbery, shooting had erupted, and the outlaws had killed four of the town's citizens, including a little girl.

According to plan, the outlaws came galloping back. Sam threw a pair of moneybags across the saddle of the oldest brother as their guard whipped the boys' horses into a run.

Scarcely knowing what was going on, the oldest of the three brothers galloped on ahead, yelling for the other two to follow him toward the river. Abject fear was working to sober the young men in a hurry. As they rode, the boys prayed they would be able to reach the river and swim the horses across before the vigilantes could overtake them.

When they realized they could not escape, they stopped their horses and were immediately surrounded by the angry townsmen. The oldest brother tried to explain what had really happened, but the vigilantes were in no mood to listen. Quickly, the mob located a tree. Ropes were brought out and nooses made. As the hangmen's ropes were tossed over the limbs, the youths begged, screamed and tried to explain, but to no avail. When the three were led on horseback to the tree and the ropes were placed around their necks, one of the boys managed to blurt out, "For God's sake, let us see our mother!"

"You can see her in Hell," one of the vigilantes shouted. With that, the horses were lashed, and a few seconds later three young bodies dangled from a huge tree limb.

Just as the three stopped struggling, the sky started turning dark, and the leaves started falling from the tree on which the boys were hanging. The leaves continued to fall until the tree was completely bare. One of the older vigilantes said, "Maybe we made a mistake. They don't look like outlaws. Why, one of them looks to be only a boy."

The bodies were cut down. By now, the mob was beginning to calm down and return to their senses. They examined the bodies for identification. Imagine their feelings of inept sorrow and distress when they discovered that they had hanged three innocent young men. The townsmen placed the bodies on horses and rode downstream to a ferry which crossed the Ohio to a point near the boys' home on the Illinois side.

After the three boys were buried, the grief-stricken mother moved away. For years after the hanging until the death of the last of the vigilantes, on still, damp nights, the sounds of galloping horses, cursing men and pleading boys' voices could be heard at the site of the still-bare hanging tree. The sounds would last for a few frightening minutes, and then all would be quiet.

Several months after the hanging the true story of the robbery was learned from a captured member of the Jackson gang.

Author's Note: This incident was kept quiet by the vigilantes and their friends. The story was not told any outsider until 1949, when the last man who had taken part of the hanging died at the age of 90. Even now I cannot disclose the real names of any of the vigilantes. The tree was still standing in 1975, but no leaves have ever grown on its branches since the day of the hanging.

Ghost Bride

In late July 1938, Martin Harmon received a telephone call at his wholesale grocery company's office in Whitesburg, Kentucky, asking him to come to Harlan, Kentucky. A coal company had opened a new commissary and wanted a complete line of groceries and tools delivered, but needed a salesman to make a list before they could place such a large order.

It was late in the day when Harmon left Whitesburg; but because the mountain roads were in poor condition and because a storm seemed imminent, he decided to leave on his trip at once. It was beginning to get dark when he reached the other side of Pine Mountain, and he found himself in a regular cloudburst. The rumbling thunder seemed to shake the mountain, and flashes of lightning created an eerie world out of the darkness. High winds hurled tree limbs and other debris into the road, slowing Harmon's progress. There was not a place within miles where he could hope to get a night's lodging...he had to keep going.

He had turned a sharp curve in the winding road when he almost lost control of his car.... There beside the road was a young woman, waving for him to stop. He could see by his headlights that she was dressed in a wedding gown!

Harmon pulled to a stop, and the girl approached the car. Her dark hair was rain soaked, and her face had a gray pallor—she seemed to be in a state of shock.

In an almost hysterical voice she told him that the bridge he would have to cross on Poor Fork of the Cumberland River had washed away in the storm...that she and a girlfriend had driven into the swollen stream, and the friend had drowned. She then told him he should not drive down into the valley but should, instead, take another road a few hundred yards ahead.

Harmon asked the girl if he could help her. She replied that her name was Coleen Tyler, that she lived on the road she knew to be safe, and she would like to ride that far.

When the young woman sat down beside him, Harmon noticed that she was developing a chill. He placed his coat around her shoulders, but she seemed not to notice. Her head was turned, and she kept looking out the window into the storm, as if searching for something or someone. Asking for directions, Harmon was told to turn on to a gravel road.

Though it continued to rain, and occasional flashes of lightning could still be seen, and the rumble of thunder came from the mountain, the worst of the storm was over. Harmon was curious about the girl, wondering why she was dressed in bridal attire and what she had been doing on this lonely mountain road at night in such a storm. He didn't question her—she seemed to still be in shock, continuing to stare vacantly out the car's window.

After about half an hour, they arrived at Coleen's home. The rain had stopped. She thanked him, and as Harmon watched her in his car's headlights, she walked around the house to what he assumed was the back door.

Harmon drove on toward Harlan before he remembered that Coleen still had his coat around her shoulders. But he was now in a hurry to continue his trip and decided to stop by on his return. The small frame house would be easy to find because it had the only white board fence he had seen along the gravel road.

The next morning in Harlan, Harmon learned that the bridge Coleen had told him about had indeed washed away during the storm of the previous night. Two men had drowned when their car ran into the stream (they had failed to see that the bridge was gone), but no one else was reported drowned. Harmon was now more than ever determined to stop and thank Coleen for her warning which had almost certainly saved his life.

After finishing his business, Harmon started on his return trip to Whitesburg, following the route Coleen had shown him. He arrived at her house within a few hours. An elderly, white-haired lady answered his knock and stared at him in disbelief as Harmon introduced himself and told her briefly of his experience of the night before.

"I am Coleen's mother," the woman said, "and you have to be mistaken. It couldn't have been my daughter because she drowned four years ago in just such a storm as we had last night. You must have seen someone else."

She explained that Coleen and a friend had been on their way to a church in the valley where Coleen was to be married. The rest of the family had already gone to the church and were waiting when the storm started. Not knowing the bridge had been washed away, the two young ladies drove their car into the river, and both were drowned. Coleen's body had been recovered and was buried in the family cemetery a short distance back of the house.

It was Harmon's turn to stare. Mrs. Tyler said, "I'll show you her grave."

Harmon remembered as they walked across the yard and around the house that Coleen had been walking this way when he last saw her. As they neared the cemetery, Mrs. Tyler continued, "Since it was to have been her wedding day, we decided to bury Coleen in her wedding gown. We thought she would have liked that."

When they came to Coleen's grave, they were both amazed and stood speechless, for there, draped over the headstone, was Harmon's coat and a still-damp bridal veil.

Author's Note: I can learn of no sighting of this phantom within the last thirty-odd years, but the ghost of the bride-to-be was seen on several occasions during the 1930s and 1940s, either near where the old bridge crossed Poor Fork of the Cumberland River, or along the road that used to pass close by this stream. The apparition was always seen during or just before a heavy rain storm.

Ghost at the Well

The following story was told to me several years ago by an old mountaineer. The farmhouse where the events took place is a perfect setting for a ghost sighting. The old, deserted house is falling down. It sits forlornly in a weed-choked yard, surrounded by ancient trees which cast shadows in the moonlight (shadows that resemble hands reaching out as if trying to stop some terrible deed), and a sagging fence whose gate long ago gave up the struggle to hang straight. It is a quiet, lonely place.

The story began in 1921 when James Adair, his wife and two small children, aged six and four, moved to southeastern Pike County, Kentucky. Adair was a quiet, hardworking man who spent most of each week away from home on his job. His wife, Velma, was just the opposite—she loved to dance and to visit neighbors. She usually spent more time socializing than she did caring for her family.

It wasn't long before two of the local young men began to take advantage of Adair's absence to visit Velma on one pretense or another. At first no gossip was attached to the attention being paid to the young wife and mother; but when the visits of the two men began to be every night when Adair wasn't home, rumors started to circulate in the hill country.

As usually happens, someone dropped a word to Adair during one of his weekends at home. Most people thought this would be the end of it.... Adair would talk to his wife and put a stop to the visits. But he appeared to ignore the gossip.

Adair took several days off from his job so he and a few neighbors could start digging a well in his backyard. When the shaft was down to 40 feet, they struck water, which filled the well to a depth of about 20 feet.

A few days later, Adair's nearest neighbors were summoned by his small son. They rushed to the house and found Adair on his knees, looking into the well, where his wife's body was floating. He later explained that he had not had time to build a covering for the well opening. He had been tired and had gone to bed early the night before and went straight to sleep...he had not missed his wife until morning. She must have gone outside during the night, he said, and in the dark, accidentally stumbled into the well and drowned.

There was no reason to disbelieve Adair's story...several of the men present had helped him dig the well. They understood that with all of the other work Adair had to do, he simply had not had time to build a covering.

The large gash on Velma's head was believed to have been made by the rock wall of the well. No autopsy was performed—the coroner returned the verdict of "death by accident."

One thing did seem strange though. A gold locket and chain, Velma's most prized piece of jewelry, which she was never known to remove from her neck, was missing. But those things get lost; it was probably at the bottom of the well. It could have broken when she fell.

A few months later, after Adair and his children had moved away, those who passed the deserted house at night reported seeing a ghost. The pale figure of a woman was seen walking in the yard then disappearing into the well. Screams would be heard, as if from a great distance. After a few such sightings several people in the little community began to recall various strange things that had happened after Velma's death.

Adair had been extremely nervous and insisted on burying his wife almost immediately after the inquest. He would let no one talk to his children.

Less than a week after his wife's funeral, Adair sold almost everything he owned and moved away, telling no one where he was going.

Several weeks after Velma's funeral, a blood-spotted crowbar and a gold locket and chain, exactly like Velma's, were found by a road crew working less than a mile from Adair's home.

And the two young men who had visited Velma so frequently left the neighborhood suddenly. "They joined the Army," their families explained.

The hill people wondered about these things and now suspected that Adair had killed his wife. But since Velma had no relatives to press further investigation, and since there was no real proof, nothing more was done.

Though the mysterious death of Velma Adair occurred over sixty years ago, there are those who have visited the deserted farmhouse recently. Even now, they say, when the moon is full and winds are chasing clouds across the sky, when the air is brisk with autumn, the pale, misty outline of a woman, who is dressed in a long white nightgown and who has a terrible wound on her head, can be seen in the half shadows cast by the ancient trees that surround the old dwelling. The apparition holds its throat and walks around the yard looking down, as if searching. After a few seconds it drifts slowly along the ground to the old well, where it disappears. Then, the screams are heard, screams which gradually fade into silence.

Strangely, the apparition has never been seen to come out of the well. It just appears suddenly in the yard, and the screams are not heard until it disappears. This phenomenon has been witnessed many times by many different people during the last sixty years.

I visited the farm at night and saw the house and partially filled well. For those who are faint-of-heart, the old, deserted farmhouse is no place to be during the "witching hour."

Since most ghost stories are shrouded in mystery and do not have to be proved, one view is as accurate as another. But one thing is certain. There are more mysteries than known facts. There will always be something to keep us puzzled.

Spencer County Ghost Dog

The three of us had been to Wakefield, the Spencer County town where the infamous Civil War leader, William Quantrill, was shot in 1865. I was with William Metcalf and a schoolteacher, whose name now escapes me, that day in 1975. We were returning to Louisville after doing some research on the Quantrill affair.

Just after we had passed Taylorsville, we saw a large German shepherd dog standing near the middle of the road. The animal was standing over what appeared to be a man's hat,

Author stands in curve of road where a ghost dog has been seen numerous times.

as if he were protecting it. Thinking that there might have been an accident, we stopped our car and got out to investigate. As we looked back, the dog and the hat simply disappeared. Mystified, we searched along the road but were unable to find anything that we could relate to the incident. After a few minutes, we gave up our efforts and continued our journey back to Louisville.

I was more than somewhat surprised several days later when another friend told me just about the same story. He, too, had seen a dog guarding a hat on the same road. In fact, his description fit the same location as the place where we had seen the strange happening. This friend had also stopped to investigate, and both the dog and hat vanished.

It was weeks later when I had occasion to again be driving this road in Spencer County. As I approached the spot where we had first seen the dog and the hat, I wasn't really surprised when I saw it again. There was the dog, standing over a tan felt hat. When I stopped the car and got out, the dog and hat again disappeared. It occurred to me that the time was about the same as when I first witnessed the event. It was about two o'clock in the afternoon and was on Thursday in each case. Ghosts are usually reported as having been seen at night or dusk at the earliest. Because of this added, unusual dimension, I determined that I wanted to learn more about this ghost dog with the unusual schedule.

I drove on down the road several hundred yards and stopped at the first farmhouse that I came to. An elderly lady answered my knock. I apologized for the intrusion, then asked if I might talk with her about my experience with the dog and hat. She listened patiently, then explained that I was not the first to see the dog and hat at the curve in the road. In fact, she pointed out that several folks had been witness to the scene. She concluded by giving me the only explanation she had for the appearance of the apparition.

The lady told me that about 10 years earlier, a farmer named McKinney was walking along the road. His dog, a German shepherd, was walking with him. At the curve, both the man and the dog were struck and killed by a hit-and-run driver. The driver of the car was never apprehended. I asked her if she knew the day and time of the accident that claimed the life of the man and his dog. For some reason, I was not at all surprised when she replied, "About two o'clock on a Thursday afternoon."

Callahan and the Phantom Horse

Relatives of Dennis Callahan still tell the story of his terrible death in 1930. A few older members of that eastern Kentucky family still recall the frightening, unexplainable details of the event.

Callahan was a man of violent temper. He owned a large farm and worked a great number of farm animals. Without exception, he treated them cruelly. A horse or mule that didn't perform exactly as Callahan expected was savagely beaten with a heavy whip which he always carried. He appeared to take special delight in whipping one bay horse in particular. At the slightest provocation, Callahan would whip the bay until blood ran from the cuts.

Once a neighbor told him, "Someday you'll pay for the way you treat that animal." But Callahan only laughed.

In July 1910, Callahan whipped the horse so badly that it bled to death. Two farmhands who witnessed the beating swore that just before the horse died, they saw hate in the animal's eyes...hate such as they had never before seen from a dumb animal. The body of the horse was thrown into a sinkhole on the farm.

After thirty years of prosperous farming, Callahan had become financially well off for the times. He sold his farm and bought a house at the edge of a nearby town. In back of the house was a large field where the man kept several fox hounds. The incident of the bay horse and its bloody death twenty years earlier had long since been put out of his mind.

One day in 1930, Callahan went into the field to check on his hounds. Later, his wife said that her first indication that something was wrong came when she heard the excited barking of the dogs. This was soon followed by frantic screams from her husband. He was shouting, "For God's sake, somebody get this horse away from me!"

Mrs. Callahan ran to the edge of the field where she could see her husband running in circles. He was dodging and running as if to avoid an attacker...an attacker that Mrs. Callahan could not see. Each time Dennis Callahan stumbled and fell, she could see his clothing sink as from an invisible blow. Each time the mysterious force struck him, blood spurted from the wound it made. Above the commotion of her husband's screams and the bark of the dogs. Mrs. Callahan could hear the shrill whinny of a horse and the sound of stomping horse hooves.

The noise had drawn several neighbors to the field. They too, could hear the sounds of an enraged horse but could not see one. After several minutes, Callahan lay motionless in a trampled and bloody mass. At this point, the sounds of the horse stopped, as if the invisible avenger realized that its antagonist was dead.

Mrs. Callahan and her neighbors watched as the doctor and county coroner examined the dead man. They found that most every bone in Callahan's body had been broken. On his body they found numerous imprints of a horseshoe although not one hoofprint could be found on the ground. There was no evidence of trampled grass or broken shrubbery that might have been caused by a horse. There was nothing to indicate that a horse had ever been in the field.

The autopsy performed on Callahan's body turned up a most unusual finding—mixed with the human blood was the blood of a horse! Impossible? There are persons still alive today who can remember the day Dennis Callahan was trampled to death by an invisible horse. They will swear that the event took place just the way it has been related. Is it possible that the bay horse Callahan had beaten to death twenty years before somehow came back to wreak this terrible revenge on the man who had killed it?

Confederate Ghost
of Frozen Creek

Several years ago, an historical marker stood along the Mountain Parkway near Jackson, Kentucky. I have yet to learn why it was removed. The marker stated that a young Confederate scout named Spencer was chased down and killed by Union sympathizers, or bushwhackers, while riding near the home of his parents. His killers were never caught or identified.

It was along the old road, at the left of this stream, where the young Confederate soldier's ghost was seen in 1942.

Young Spencer had come home on military leave from his Confederate unit. To avoid being seen by any who might be unfriendly to his cause, he had waited until after dark to slip quietly in through the back door of his parents' home. After resting two days, he decided to visit his girlfriend, whose family lived on Big Frozen Creek. The first visit was uneventful, but on the third night, young Spencer took his father's saddle horse and started for his girlfriend's home again. When he came to the point where a small stream empties into Big Frozen Creek, the bushwhackers were waiting for him. His attackers cut his throat, tied him on his horse and whipped the animal back in the direction of his parents' home. By the time he arrived, the young soldier had bled to death.

It was a few years after the Civil War had ended before people started to tell about seeing the ghost of a Confederate soldier galloping on horseback down the creek. Those who told the story always said that the ghost-soldier was tied to the saddle, his feet out of the stirrups, blood streaming from a terrible gash in his throat and that he appeared to be looking back in horror as if watching for his pursuers. This apparition was seen on many occasions until the beginning of World War II. For some reason, it has not been seen since that time.

Ghosts on the Mississippi

Perhaps you have heard stories of the cruel and inhuman methods used by some plantation owners to break unruly black slaves prior to the Civil War. There have been stories of beating, starving, shooting and even burning; but for outright disregard for human life and suffering, the following story is probably the worst example of inhumane treatment I have encountered.

Having heard of my interest in unusual and unexplainable events, Jonathan Allen of Hickman, Kentucky, contacted me. He invited me to visit, saying that he could relate several interesting stories and would be happy to show me where they had occurred. On a trip to western Kentucky, I spent some twelve enjoyable and fascinating hours with Mr. Allen. He is extremely well versed in local folklore and history. He

Scene along the Mississippi River.

has spent years on the Mississippi River and can relate countless tales of strange happenings along that fabled stream. Not only did he tell me the following story...he also took me to the exact location where the incident is said to have occurred in 1817.

In 1806 the Congress of the United States passed a law declaring it illegal to import Negroes into this country for the purpose of selling them. Defying the law, many white traders made fortunes dealing in contraband slaves. The Negroes were captured or bought from their own countrymen in Africa, shipped to Cuba or other Caribbean islands, then placed on boats and smuggled into the United States. This trafficking continued until the start of the Civil War.

In July 1817 a boat left Cuba bound for the Mississippi River. On board were twelve Negroes, shackled and bound. Skirting the Gulf mainland, the ship reached the Mississippi Delta. The journey upriver was made primarily at night. During the daylight hours, the ship hid along the bayous and tributaries. The ship and crew were nearing their destination in western Kentucky when they were intercepted by a federal patrol boat. Realizing that they would face a possible prison sentence and fine in addition to losing their human cargo if they allowed themselves to be caught with the slaves, the ship's masters chose another way out.

They had the crew herd the terrified blacks on deck. Each of the slaves was bound by an iron collar around his neck. Each collar was attached to a connecting chain so that all twelve were tied together. Crew members took the trailing end of the slave chain and attached it to a large anchor. The anchor was dragged to the side of the ship and dropped overboard. The federal agents on the patrol boat could only watch helplessly. They were too far away to stop the deed.

It is almost impossible even to imagine the terror the victims must have felt when they realized what was happening...that escape was impossible. The weight of the anchor was too much for the chained slaves to resist. One by one they were pulled over the side and into the water, each one adding more weight to the chain that was pulling the struggling, screaming drudges to a watery grave. The federal agents were helpless and could do nothing to the ship's crew without evidence, and all the evidence was at the bottom of the Mississippi.

This tragic event took place on a lonely stretch of the Mississippi River southwest of Hickman. Mr. Allen says that even today folks can still hear the screams of those drowning slaves sometimes when the bright moonlight displays the pale outline of a ship in the night and the river moves with strange sounds that most folks would rather not talk about.

Ghost Legions at Doctor's Creek

The Civil War has always interested me because so many unexplained incidents took place during that period. It seems that events of the era have even extended beyond their place in time. I was a witness to such an event in July 1972. I was visiting the Perryville Battlefield in Boyle County. Given the

It was to the right (in the field) of the Confederate Monument that I heard the sounds of running soldiers.

facts that this is the site of the largest Civil War engagement fought in Kentucky and that several thousand men died here in a single afternoon, this area is fertile ground for ghosts and other unexplained phenomena.

Prior to my visit in 1972, I had hiked through the area with a farmer named Hampton who lived near the battlefield. As we walked he told me that sometimes at night one could hear cannon and rifle fire coming from the vicinity of the old battlefield. On some particularly dark and damp night, folks had even seen muzzle flashes in connection with the sounds. He told me that at the time of the battle, the area had been covered with timber with only a single wagon road traversing what is now the battle site. Practically all evidence of the battle, even the old road, is gone now. Only a few monuments commemorate the bloody struggle that took place in 1862.

Several days after my visit with Mr. Hampton, I attended the outdoor drama, *The Legend of Daniel Boone,* at the amphitheater in Harrodsburg. When the drama was over, I noticed that there was a full moon. It occurred to me that it would be fascinating to see the Perryville Battlefield at night and by bright moonlight. I drove the ten or so miles, parked my car and got out. I walked around the area near the battlefield, seeing only cleared land and the distant timberline as a dark backdrop. Below the fields was the shadowy outline of Doctor's Creek. At first the only sounds I could hear were the buzzing of insects and the occasional call of a whippoorwill. It was so quiet and peaceful that it was hard to imagine the area had ever been witness to such violence and carnage that claimed so many lives.

As I neared the old ford in Doctor's Creek, where so many soldiers on both sides met death, I heard something. It started as a faint, far-off rumble...the muffled sound of distant, running feet. At first I thought my imagination was playing tricks on me, but the sound came closer and grew louder. The sound was now more discernible...running feet...hundreds or even thousands of them, running through dry leaves. But there were no dry leaves! The intensity of the sound increased until I was surrounded by it. I could also hear the heavy breathing of the runners and the clank of equipment, but I could see nothing...not even movement in the dark. The sounds continued for several minutes and then were gone...a low rumble on the wind. I don't mind telling you, it took a while longer for the hair on the back of my neck to lay down!

When all was quiet again, I looked down at the ground to make sure that there were no dry leaves, swinging my foot from side to side. There were none...not on this clear, moonlit night in July.

At the first opportunity following my experience, I studied some of the old records dealing with the Battle of Perryville. I learned that several companies of Confederate soldiers, camped 16 miles away at Mackville, had double-timed to Perryville in an attempt to turn the tide of the battle. The engagement, indecisive for either side, took place on October 7 and 8, 1862, after a long, dry summer, which had caused the leaves to fall early. An old military map of the area indicated that I had been standing directly in the path that the double-timing relief column had taken...the wagon road that crossed Doctor's Creek!

Ohio River Phantoms

Most all American rivers have their peculiar tales of tragedy, replete with ghosts, strange sounds and unexplained events. But for sheer numbers of eerie stories, the Ohio River probably tops them all.

From Pittsburgh, Pennsylvania, to Cairo, Illinois, I have heard fishermen and boaters relate a veritable cornucopia of tales that seem to touch every one of the Ohio's 981 miles. Many of these legends date back to early settlement time and were never recorded...except in legend.

One of the strangest tales I have heard concerns the ghosts of victims killed by river pirates operating near Cave-

Scene along the Ohio River.

in-Rock, Illinois. I am told that on still, dark nights when fog rises from the river, the ghostly outline of a flatboat can be seen floating silently downstream. The faint lapping of oars in the water can be heard as unseen rowers move swiftly to intercept the flatboat and its ghostly passengers in a special reenactment of robbery and murder consummated long ago in the dim, distant past. Sometimes the voices of those who died seem to float on the wind. At other times voices pleading for mercy, screaming in pain and fear, can be heard. Reliable historians estimate that more than 100 people were killed on the Ohio River in the vicinity of Cave-in-Rock between 1790 and 1820.

Other sections of the Ohio claim their share of frightful episodes. I have been told of a family, who was killed by Indians near present-day Augusta, Kentucky, while travelling down the Ohio in a flatboat. The father was scalped alive, the mother was taken captive, two slaves were killed and three children drowned. Indian war whoops and screams of the victims can still be heard some nights. There are those who report having seen flashes from guns near the middle of the river.

Near the mouth of the Kentucky River, where it empties into the Ohio, folks have seen a phantasm involving two steamboats. Those having witnessed the apparition say there is a collision and explosion. From amidst the smoke and confusion that follows, they hear screams of pain and wild thrashing in the water, as if passengers were trying to escape the burning vessels and swim ashore. The phenomenon lasts for a few minutes, and then all is again quiet.

The death of an Indian squaw and her three children at the hands of white men is the basis for another spectre that has haunted many Ohio River travellers. In 1781 three white men waited to ambush Indians that might be crossing the Ohio near the present location of Maysville, Kentucky. As it happened, an Indian mother and her children were fishing in the river. Their canoe drifted past the white men's hiding place. The men fired at the canoe, killing the three children with their first volley. The mother tried desperately to paddle the canoe out of range, but the oar was broken in her frenzied effort. The canoe started drifting back toward the Kentucky side as the three men reloaded their weapons. Although she must have realized the hopelessness of the situation, the woman raised her arms in supplication and began pleading for her life in her native tongue. Taking careful aim, the three men shot the woman, leaving the canoe to float on downriver with the four dead bodies. For years after this senseless killing, the pale outline of a large canoe with three dead Indian children hanging over the sides and the pleading mother on her knees with her arms raised could be seen on still, damp nights, floating down the middle of the Ohio.

The Headless Timberman

The ghost of the headless timberman has been seen on both sides of this old abandoned road.

During the timber cutting days of 1885 to 1910, a sawmill where dozens of men were employed sat beside a certain old gravel road in Estill County. The hands' entertainment at day's end was playing cards, pitching horseshoes and telling stories. One night, just after payday, a poker game was in progress. Moonshine was flowing freely, and what started as a friendly argument turned into a fight. During the yelling, swearing and scuffling, one of the men grabbed a large knife and started swinging wildly. The melee came to a sudden halt when the knife wielder's frenzied slashing beheaded one of the men. The others said the headless man ran down the road from the bunkhouse for about 100 feet before he fell.

Several years after the incident, a farmer was driving a

wagon along this road, when a man without a head jumped in front of his team. The terrified animals ran away with the wagon. Luckily the farmer jumped to safety. Thereafter, the apparition was seen almost nightly by those using this road.

On one occasion, a group of young people, returning home from a dance, were amazed to see a headless body, blood streaming from a horrible stump of a neck, standing before them. Scared witless, the group scattered in all directions. The apparition began to chase three girls, who ran down the road. One of the young women fell and broke her arm. She said later that the apparition passed directly over her, but she felt only what seemed to be a breeze. Later that night, the group gathered at one of their homes. After calming the young people, several fathers, armed with shotguns and carrying lanterns, walked the entire stretch of road but neither saw nor heard anything unusual.

The latest known sighting of this apparition was in August 1978. John Rose, a farmer who lived in the vicinity of this old and little used road, had gone to the grocery store, about three miles from his farm. Returning home, his car just stopped, although it had recently been serviced and should have been in good condition. When Rose got out to see if he could get it started, he saw what he first thought to be a white cow standing beside the road. The animal, or whatever it was, was making a long gasping sound, like a person smothering; then it moved toward him.

The only weapon Rose carried was a pocketknife. Backing up a few steps, he managed to get the knife out and open it. The moon was bright and, when the apparition (he could see now that it was not an animal) started to follow him with outstretched arms, Rose realized that he had come face to face with the ghost of the headless logger. Rose is made of stern stuff and does not scare easily. He is a quiet, sober farmer not given to foolishness or superstition. He told me that he made up his mind in a second that he would be damned if a ghost or anything else was going to scare him into running to some neighbor's house for help.

Rose swears that when the apparition grabbed him around

the waist, he could actually feel a body against his. He stabbed it in the chest several times. All the while he could hear long gasping sounds coming from whatever he was fighting. After a few minutes the apparition released him and ran into the woods.

After the attack, Rose walked a half mile to a neighbor's home. The neighbor later described Rose's condition to me. "Damned if he didn't look like a stuck hog...blood was all over him, and his left arm was cut in several places." Rose was taken to a hospital where his wounds were treated. Some cuts were so severe that stitches were required.

I have looked at the scars on the left arm of John Rose. They are very real, and beyond any doubt he tangled with something...something that also must have been real. I have walked this old road, and I have seen the spot where the sawmill stood...where the headless logger staggered down the road and fell. It is a quiet, lonely place, and no one or nothing accosted me as I retraced the steps of John Rose and others before him.

The Room Upstairs

By vocation I am a treasure hunter. I use a metal detector, and old houses are among my favorite places to search. My travels have led me to many strange and unusual houses, happenings and people. While some of the houses searched seemed perfectly normal, still others seemed to be attended by spirits of another world. One of the weirdest things to ever befall me happened in 1968 while I was visiting a friend near Hardinsburg, Kentucky. This friend suggested that we search an old abandoned log house. Local legend claimed the cabin to be haunted by a screaming woman. This ghost was reportedly heard, and occasionally even seen, at night in or around the cabin.

My Breckinridge County host, my son Michael, and I took a metal detector and a rifle with us and set out for the old house about noon on a Sunday. First, we searched the yard and found nothing of value. We then went inside, where we saw pieces of old furniture, broken glass and other debris usually associated with houses long abandoned. We looked under old moldering carpets, along the walls and in the fireplace. We found nothing on the bottom floor, so we started up a rickety flight of stairs. On the top step, I lifted a piece of old linoleum. Under the linoleum was a ring. Examination revealed that it was probably a gold wedding band, and the size indicated that it belonged to a woman. I attached no special significance to the item. I have found many other more unusual things in more than 30 years of treasure hunting. I dropped it into my pocket and proceeded to search the room to my right. I found a few items and started on to the room on the opposite side.

At the doorway to the second room, I felt a rush of cold

air, although the temperature outside was in the 90s. It seemed I could also hear faint voices coming from the room. I could not make out the words, but it sounded like a man and a woman arguing. I made a move to enter the door, and as I did, I could feel pressure against my chest as if a hand were blocking my way. The touch was light but sufficiently firm to keep me back. I made three more attempts to walk through the door, and each time was denied entrance by the unseen hand. My son Michael was standing there the last couple of times that I tried to enter, and he could see an indentation on my shirt each time. Both Michael and our host could walk freely in and out of the room, and neither of them heard the faint voices that I had heard.

After making a total of five attempts to enter the room, I asked Michael to hand me the rifle. I took the weapon and pumped 15 rounds into the room, breaking glass, plaster and creating havoc in general. Then, twice more I tried to go through the door, but the unseen hand still pushed me back. Mike and our friend then suggested it was time for us to leave.

We took our leave of our friends and returned home. I put the incident out of my mind. It was not until some two years later that I recalled the visit to the old cabin and the wedding band I had found there. The occasion for the remembrance was a visit from a woman psychic from Ohio. I told her nothing about the ring or the circumstances under which I had acquired it. I merely handed her the ring and asked if she could tell me anything about it. Barely had the ring touched her hand when she threw it to the floor.

"There's blood on it!" she exclaimed. "It feels like it's on fire! The woman who wore that ring is dead, killed by a blow to the head. She was murdered by her husband and her body was hidden."

At the time when I handed the ring to the psychic, I had no idea about who had owned the ring...if the person was dead or alive...married or unmarried.

Several weeks later I was back in Hardinsburg again. I looked up the man who owned the property where the old cabin stood. He told me that, about 30 years earlier, a man and his wife had lived in the big log house. One morning the man came to see the present landowner and advised him that he could have the farm if he would take it and pay the taxes. The man said he was leaving and would not be coming back. Sure enough, he was never seen again.

Shortly after the man had left, folks began to hear screams around the old house at night. Some said they saw a woman in a long gown running across the yard. After several reports of the screams and apparitions, county officials came to investigate. Under the floor of one room in the cabin, they found the skeleton of a woman dressed in the remnants of a long nightgown. A wrist watch found with the skeleton and dental records provided sufficient proof that the skeleton was that of the former landowner's wife. Although the police spent years searching, the dead woman's husband was never located.

It seems strange that the screams have not been heard, neither has the figure in the long gown been seen, since I found the ring over 12 years ago.

All that remains (in 1979) of the old log cabin where I could not enter an upstairs room.

Wailing Woman of Warrior's Path

During the period from 1774 to 1792, a Warrior's Path used by Indians raiding white settlers in Kentucky ran from the Scioto River in Ohio to various points south of the Ohio River. Hundreds of isolated cabins were scattered throughout the eastern half of the territory that was to become the Commonwealth of Kentucky.

In one such dwelling lived Mr. and Mrs. William Grange and their two small daughters. They were among the first colonists from Maryland to settle in Kentucky.

Grange was away from home in August 1789, when an Indian war party raided his cabin. Mrs. Grange saw the savages coming up the trail and managed to hurry the children out the back door. They ran toward a cave in a nearby hill, hoping they could hide there until the Indians went away. Before they could reach the cave, one of the Indians spotted the trio and alerted his companions. The war party caught up to the fleeing family and brutally grabbed them.

One of the Indians picked up the youngest daughter and bashed her head against a tree, while the other shot and scalped Mrs. Grange. The oldest of the daughters was taken captive. After murdering Mrs. Grange and her youngest daughter, the Indians set fire to the cabin and watched it burn. When Grange returned and learned what had happened to his family, the shock was so great that he nearly went mad. He returned to Maryland where he soon died...some say largely from grief. The surviving daughter was eventually ransomed from the Indians and returned to tell of the raid.

It was about five years after the death of the Granges when a ghostly presence first manifested itself in the area where the cabin had stood. In 1794 a hunter was startled by a ghostly voice coming from a point on the hillside near the Grange cabin site. The hunter said the voice sounded like someone in distress calling for help. It lasted only a few moments and then died away. The hunter searched for the source of the voice but could find nothing. A few weeks later two other hunters were in the same area. As they sat by their campfire one night, they heard a strange sound which they thought might be the cry of a wildcat or panther. The wild and weird sounds lasted nearly an hour, gradually diminishing to an occasional sob, then stopping altogether.

In the year 1800, a man named Owen built a cabin on nearly the exact spot where the Grange cabin had stood. Owen had heard the story of the strange, wailing voice but insisted that the hunters were just imagining things or making up stories. One night, after the Owen family had been living in their new cabin for several weeks, they heard the strange cry. Mr. Owen yelled back, asking the voice to identify itself and its purpose in calling. The voice then became clearer...identifiable as that of a woman wailing, "Come here! Come here! Help me! Help me!" The entire mountain seemed filled with the sobbing cries of the ghostly voice. After about two hours, the cries stopped. The Owen family was unable to sleep much that night because of their strange experience. The next morning they took their belongings and moved from the area.

Like its predecessor, the old Owen cabin is now gone, too. Local folks still avoid the area on the stream where the cabins stood. There is no road up this creek, but campers occasionally come into the area. As recently as 1980, a group of backpackers hiking in the area heard the scream of a woman pleading for someone to come and help her.

Woman in Black

The following is from a letter I received from a lady in Floyd County, Kentucky:

"Most ghost stories are hand-me-downs and proven false. But this one happened many years ago and is as true as gospel. When my husband and I were young, we lived on a widow's farm. They went on a trip and got us to stay as care-takers in the big nine-room house. It was in the wintertime.

"One midnight we heard a loud beating on the front door. We at once thought of robbers, knowing the valuable things the house contained. After the knocking stopped we heard a woman's footsteps on the long side porch. We thought she was going to the side door, but she stopped at the big bay window and shook it violently. I said, 'Who is there and what do you want?' My husband told me to be still. By the moon-light reflected on snow and a fire in the grate, we plainly saw a form wearing a long black dress.

"We slept no more that night and got up early the next morning. We went to both porches to pick up footprints in the two or three inches of snow that had fallen the day before. But there were no footprints in any direction. That stumped us. We knew that footprints should have been left by anyone making that much noise at the front door and bay window.

"The next day I went to town and saw a woman in a store who had once lived on the same place. I told her what we had heard and seen the night before. She said, 'That place is haunted. The old man who died there had cheated his only sister out of her share. She told him she'd come back and haunt the place. She always wears a long black dress.'

"I grabbed the counter in fright. 'Ooh,' I said, 'when we saw her she was wearing black!' The woman then told me that

The old house where the ghost of a woman, wearing a long black dress, has been seen.

others had stayed in the old place as caretakers. One such couple had two little girls sleeping in an upstairs room when the form came, wearing a black dress, and pulled their covers off. One little girl fainted, and the other fell down the stairs and broke her arm.

"It was also in this house that a closet door could not be kept locked. My husband once nailed it shut, but the next morning it was wide open. Well, I went back to the house, but we shortly moved away from there. The old house is still standing; I always get a scared, creepy feeling when I pass it."

I have no reason to question this lady's integrity. There is no doubt in my mind that she and her husband saw and heard something they could not explain.

Runaway Ghosts

During the 1920s, a wagon drawn by a team of horses or mules was the common means of transportation in eastern Kentucky. In those days it was customary to hitch a team with a halter rope when the wagon was stopped. This was particularly true if the animals were young or not sufficiently trained.

Stephen Ledbetter was visiting his neighbor, William Thacker. Their farms joined and the two friends often shared work as well as leisure time. Ledbetter had driven to the Thacker farm in a light spring wagon drawn by a pair of young and spirited mules. The road that connected the two farms ran along the side of a hill. At one point the road was as much as fifty feet above the river. The riverbed below and the bank leading down to the water were strewn with jagged rocks that had fallen from the cliffs above the road.

When Ledbetter arrived, he hitched his team and joined his friend in the back yard. He could not see the wagon, but felt secure in the knowledge that he had hitched the team securely. After a few minutes of conversation, the men heard some of the children scream, accompanied by the sound of a moving wagon. Immediately, they ran toward the sound, and as they reached the front yard, they saw Thacker's two young sons, aged eight and ten, on Ledbetter's wagon. The youngsters, in an apparent attempt to mimic their elders, had unhitched the team and climbed onto the wagon. The young mules, sensing something unusual, became excited and started running. The two inexperienced boys sat huddled together in fear, instead of jumping from the wagon before the mules had time to get up speed.

Without a man's strong hand on the reins, the mules were

soon galloping at full speed. Ledbetter and Thacker ran as fast as they could, shouting for the team to stop, but to no avail...the mules kept right on running up the narrow road beside the river. Several hundred yards from the house the team reached the crest of the hill. It was here that the front axle broke. The wagon lurched and went flying into space as it left the roadway. Downward the wagon plummeted, taking the team and the two young boys to horrible deaths on the jagged rocks 50 feet below. By the time Ledbetter and Thacker reached the spot, there was nothing but the mangled remains of the two children, the two mules and the spring wagon that had carried them to their deaths.

A few nights after the incident, haunting screams were heard from the hillside. The travellers who heard the screams said they also saw the ghostly outline of two fiery-eyed mules pulling a spring wagon with two young boys frantically clutching the seat. The apparition first appeared on the road; then it floated out over the gorge and disappeared.

Until the road was finally closed and the county had built one in another location, this phenomenon was seen many times. Even today, some fox hunters walking along the ridge above the old roadbed have reported seeing a wagon and team of mules running in the moonlight. They hear terrified screams as the wagon floats off the road and disappears into the rock-strewn ravine below.

Mysterious Voices at Brent Cabin

In southcentral Kentucky there is an isolated stream where disembodied voices can be heard. These "bodiless" voices have been heard by dozens of people throughout the past 140 years at different times of the day and night and have even been captured on a tape recorder.

The earliest known record of the ghostly voices was in 1840 when a farmer named Joseph Caudill went squirrel hunting along the stream. He returned home and told his family that he had heard voices but had seen no one. Several members of his family went to the location, where they also heard the voices. The voices seemed to be all around them but in no one particular spot, and they never saw anyone. The Caudills told others, and the story spread. Since then, the voices have been heard hundreds of time by many different people.

The voices seem to be those of several people all talking at once. Some people say that the voices are trying to tell of some terrible event. Hysterical female voices have been reported mixed with those of shouting males, seemingly begging for help. At other times the sounds are soft, as if one is outside a room listening to a group of people talking normally. All reports say that the voices can be heard, but individual words cannot be distinguished. Sometimes they last for an hour, while at other times, only a few minutes. The voices are a reality. I recorded the sounds on tape. By searching county records, I think I may have found the origin of this strange phenomenon, but the reason for it remains a mystery.

There is a deed to the property dated June 2, 1827. It conveys title to Jacob Brent. He built a seven-room log cabin on it. There were 11 Brents, all considered by neighbors to be somewhat strange. They never visited anyone and discouraged anyone from visiting them. They never went to church or attended any social functions. None of the children ever married, and only seldom did any of them leave the cabin. On several occasions, hunters reported hearing weird screams and shouts coming from the direction of the cabin. There was also a sickening, sweet smell in the area. The Brents' arrival closely paralleled the beginning of strange occurrences in the neighborhood.

On one occasion, an unusual animal was killed a few miles from the Brent cabin. The hunters who shot this creature first thought it was human. It stood eight feet tall with extremely long arms and was covered with hair, except for its face. The same sweet, sickening odor that surrounded the Brent cabin permeated the air around the animal. When the creature charged, the hunters fired simultaneously. The hunters examined the dead creature and found it be female. A long gold chain with a locket was around its neck, and William Rose, a member of the hunting party, swore that the locket belonged to his daughter, who had disappeared a few weeks before. The hunters backtracked the creature straight to the Brent cabin, but the Brents denied any knowledge of it.

At another time several people saw a large bird with a wingspan estimated at 20 feet. People who saw it flying low swore that it had a human face; and each time it was seen, it was either coming from or going toward the Brent cabin.

Cliff Johnson, a well-known hunter and farmer of the area, lived about five miles from the Brents. He told of stopping at the Brent cabin once to get a drink of water and visit with them while on a hunting trip. The family was unfriendly and discouraged him from staying. Johnson swore that he saw a child with two heads playing beside the cabin with a two-legged dog that walked upright. The child and dog were quickly taken out of sight by a member of the family, who realized Johnson had seen them. Johnson left after a few minutes, and, as he went down the creek, he could hear weird screams and shouts mixed with a dog's terrified howling coming from the cabin. He never went back.

These were not the only strange animals seen in the area. One farmer shot a hog that had eight legs. Another reported seeing a goat-like creature with an upper body like that of a man. That creature reportedly attacked the farmer's cattle with a knife. The farmer shot it, but it got away. A cow that weighed an estimated three tons was seen crashing through the woods, running as if in great terror. One hysterical housewife told neighbors about seeing children, 12 inches tall, playing in a stream near her home. Others reported seeing huge snakes of species unknown to the area. Most alarming were the dozen local children who disappeared over a three-year period.

The few times that the Brents were questioned about the strange creatures and occurrences, they either denied them with no comment or contended that the persons who claimed to have seen them were imagining things.

On April 10, 1837, several families saw what appeared to be a large ball of light in the nighttime sky. The light made several circles around a radius of about 10 miles, then went in the direction of the Brent cabin and disappeared. Because so many strange things had occurred in the neighborhood, the phenomenon aroused little curiosity. A few days after the light was seen, a farmer named John Taylor and his three sons went to the Brents' for the purpose of buying some cattle. As the four men rounded a curve below the cabin, they were amazed to see that where the cabin had stood, there remained nothing but the stone foundations. Upon close examination, they could tell that the dwelling had not burned but had been lifted straight up off the ground. Limbs broken from trees that grew against the cabin proved this. Brent's wagon, carriage, tools and other farm implements were still in the barns. This was apparent proof that they had not simply moved to another area. The entire Brent family was gone without a trace, including all their cattle, horses, dogs and cats. Local authorities made an intensive search but no further trace of the Brents was ever found. The report on the Brent family's strange disappearance is still on record at the sheriff's office.

Gradually, the mystery faded from the memory of local residents. The Brent farm fell into disuse, and, for the most part, folks avoided going near the place. There were no reports of any strange sounds or unusual animals for about three years after the Brents disappeared. It was 1840 when Joseph Caudill first heard the ghostly voices.

The strange disappearance of the Brents and the eventual possession of the site by the phantom voices raise many questions, but provide no answers. Could the voices be members of the Brent family trying to make contact with someone? Are the voices attempting to explain what happened to the Brents, their animals and their cabin? Was the family involved in some form of witchcraft? Did some unknown power spirit them from earth, where they are lost in a time warp they cannot escape? Are the voices seeking help in an effort to return?

Yes, there are many questions but no answers...at least not yet...only the unintelligible babble of ghostly voices to be heard by an occasional visitor to the site of the old Brent cabin.

Ghost of Booger Hollow

In 1831, a Negro uprising known in history as the Nat Turner Insurrection took place in Virginia. This insurrection caused considerable change in the way slaves were sold and treated. Fearing additional uprisings, many owners took steps to deport their most unruly slaves. One method used was to ship the blacks south to Georgia, North and South Carolina and sell them to plantation owners. The other method was to walk the slaves down roads along the Ohio River until they reached Kentucky; here some were sold if the owner could make a deal with a local farmer. Others not sold in Kentucky walked on into Tennessee, Mississippi and Alabama. There are a number of chronicles which tell of the pathetic scene as the slaves walked through the different towns. Several accounts report hearing the muffled tramp of tired, weary slaves and the clanking chains that bound them together along the darkness of country roads or unlighted streets.

Benjamin Hocking, a large landowner in northcentral Kentucky, bought one of these slaves...a slave known only as William. Although Hocking had the status of a slaveholder and was considered a successful farmer, he was not a happy man. He had little compassion for anyone, especially for blacks, and was easily provoked to uncontrollable temper. The two men made a bad combination. Although William had been bought and sold several times, his independent spirit had not been broken. There could be only one solution in the link between William and Benjamin Hocking...sooner or later one of them would die at the hand of the other.

Several days after Hocking bought him, William forgot to open the pasture gate so that the cattle could graze. When

Hocking discovered this mistake, he tied William to a post and lashed him with a whip until blood ran down his back. From then on, Hocking administered this treatment at the slightest provocation.

In September of 1858, William had been at the Hocking farm for about two months. Hocking started to whip him again for some infraction, but this time William decided he'd had enough of this treatment. He grabbed an ax and killed Hocking. Not knowing where to go or what to do, William hid out in the woods near the farm.

When the sheriff learned that William had killed his master, he formed a posse. Bloodhounds quickly tracked down the fugitive, and William was placed in jail. That night about 50 armed white men came to the jail and demanded that William be turned over to them. Leaders of the mob told the sheriff that they did not want to chance a slave uprising in the neighborhood. The sheriff, a slave owner himself, offered no resistance.

The men took William outside of town near a creek bank, where they tied him to a tree. In spite of his pleading, they beat him to death with heavy leather straps. After making sure he was dead, they threw William's body into a sinkhole. A number of other slaves had been forced to witness William's punishment as an example of what could happen to them if they were not obedient. The slaves were ordered to make no attempt to recover William's body and to stay completely away from the area.

Several weeks later a passing farmer was the first to hear unearthly screams and the sounds of a person being beaten. He heard the sounds as he approached the stream where William had been killed. Perhaps he thought another slave was being punished. At any rate, he stopped his wagon and walked toward the tree where William had died. He saw a Negro tied there, screaming and writhing in pain as if he was being whipped, but no one else was in sight.

After this first sighting, many others heard the screams and saw the shadowy outline of a Negro trying frantically to break the bonds that tied him to the tree. These sightings continued for over 80 years until 1945 when, for some unex-plained reason, they suddenly stopped. The sightings and sounds caused people to avoid the area, which became known as Booger Hollow.

Homecoming for Jamie Coleman

The Battle of Wild Cat Mountain would be the first test under fire for the Confederates' newly organized 1st Kentucky Cavalry. The young, untried soldiers making up the unit knew very little of war. They had heard stories about the Mexican War from fathers, uncles and grandfathers, but time had laundered those experiences to the point that these young recruits looked on them as high adventure to be eagerly anticipated. As they jauntily walked along the valley road leading to Wild Cat Mountain and their rendezvous with war, the young men joked about the predicament which forced them to march into battle. Surely, they would get horses following the coming engagement; then there would be no more tiresome marching for this cavalry unit!

Jamie Coleman was among those young men of the 1st Kentucky Cavalry. He had lied about his age in order to be accepted (although recruiters on either of the two sides didn't ask for a lot of proof). He was just a boy, and he had slipped away from home to volunteer. After just a few short weeks of training, Jamie and the other young cavalrymen of the 1st Kentucky were about to learn firsthand that war is anything but an experience to eagerly anticipate. For most of them, it would be the last thing they would learn.

The 1st Kentucky began its attack in the afternoon of October 21, 1861. Quickly, the young troopers learned that bullets respect no one. As comrades fell around them, the inexperienced soldiers began to realize that they were involved in something totally different than they had envisioned when they volunteered. Now, they knew that war was less a matter of glory than a matter of survival...that war is a muster of inescapable fear and death. Amidst the din, the smoke and confusion of battle, Jamie Coleman found himself separated from his companions.

Lord, I didn't know war would be like this! The thoughts raced through his frightened mind. *All the screams, the blood and the stink is enough to make you sick. Boys I've knowed all my life dropping around me like flies. I sure wish I was home. It seems like a thousand years ago when I left. Hope I live to see Ma and Pa and the rest of the family again.*

Suddenly, the whole world seemed to explode around him. Jamie found himself directly in the path of the terrible grape shot from the cannon mounted at the top of Wild Cat Mountain. A million lights flared. There was one terrible instant of pain; then Jamie knew nothing more.

Jamie had written his parents twice after he enlisted. The first letter was filled with enthusiasm. It told of his experiences in training and the friends he had made. Fighting was still a game in his inexperienced mind, and Jamie was convinced that the Confederates would win the war in a few days. He also promised to visit home as soon as he could. Jamie's father was secretly proud of him; and, although he didn't mean it, he said, "I'll wear that youngun out with a switch when he gets home!"

Jamie's second letter showed more maturity, expressing more sober thoughts. He had begun to realize that the war might not be a picnic after all. Again he promised to visit when he could.

On October 25, 1861, Jamie's mother was working in the yard among her flowers when she saw Jamie coming up the walkway. He appeared older, and there was a faraway look in his eyes, as if he had seen things his mind could not accept. Calling his father and other members of the family, Jamie's mother hugged him as they walked into the house. The family greeted Jamie as any family would greet a returning soldier. The father promptly forgot about the whipping he was going to give his son.

That evening, neighbors gathered at the Coleman home to ask questions and discuss the battle of Wild Cat Mountain with Jamie. Jamie seemed withdrawn and reluctant to talk during the entire evening. Family and friends attributed this strange behavior to his battle experience and the fact that this was his first visit home. They felt the two events had combined to put him into a mild state of shock. Time would cure that...he was a veteran of one battle now.

For the next three days, Jamie helped his mother with chores around the house and visited friends in the neighborhood. But, as they all noticed, he had the haunted look of one who has seen too much of death and suffering not fully understood. On the fourth day, Jamie told his family, "I have to get back now. My friends over on the mountain need me." It was approaching dusk when Jamie departed. As he took leave of his mother, he seemed hardly aware of her presence, his thoughts apparently in another place. Mrs. Coleman saw him go through the gate; then he seemed to float just above the ground in the direction of Wild Cat Mountain. Later, she told friends that she thought it was her eyes or the gathering darkness that gave the impression that Jamie was drifting above the path.

It wasn't until the family learned of Jamie's death that his mother realized that the son who had visited them was of another world. Casualties of Wild Cat Mountain were officially released to the next of kin on October 30, 1861. Jamie Coleman was one of the first to die, hit by a shell during the initial charge on October 21.

House of Smoke and Fire

In southcentral Kentucky there is a haunted house. That is not so unusual...there are lots of those. However, this one was different because the owners had a standing offer to give it to anyone who would spend the night in it. A young couple has now purchased the house and is renovating it against the advice of neighbors. Only time will tell if these young people will encounter any of the demonic manifestations witnessed by others.

For years the stories have been told that no lights of any kind will burn in this house, smoke without fire fills the rooms and rumbling sounds are heard late at night.

The original owner moved out of the house over 30 years ago when these unusual signs began. Several men in the community tried to spend a night in the structure, but fear overcame bravery. The men claimed to have seen a man with large red eyes following them from room to room. They also claimed that the house shook and filled with smoke, making it impossible to breathe. Needless to say, they did not stay the night.

In 1978, three men from Ohio told the owner that for $5,000 they would spend a night in the house. He wanted to sell the property and, hoping to disprove the existence of ghosts or diabolic demonstrations, agreed to pay the three men. The men entered. All seemed normal and quiet in the large house. Although there were no steady lights, an occasional flash, as if matches were being struck, could be seen by curious people outside. About 1:00 a.m., when most of the curiosity seekers had gone home and all was still, the three men inside began screaming that they could not get out, that they were on fire and could not breathe. When the police finally broke down a door, the three men came crawling out of the house, unable to stand. Two men had white hair and seemed to have aged beyond their years, while the third man had lost nearly half his body weight and had pulled most of his hair out by the roots. All three were hopelessly insane. They were committed to an asylum, where they remain today. No one knows what terrible thing they saw.

Strangely, no noise has ever been heard and no smoke has ever been seen outside the house. These unusual events happen only when someone is inside and only at night. Another aspect of the phenomenon is that no one has ever died, naturally or unnaturally, as would be expected in happenings of this nature.

I have checked the history of this dwelling thoroughly. The building site may hold a clue to the abnormal happenings reported there. It was built within a few yards and on a direct line with a cave that extends for several miles into Pine Mountain. The Cumberland River cut through the mountain thousands of years ago, dividing this huge cavern. The part on the south side of the river can be explored today, but the northern end of this cavern was sealed by the United States government during the early 1930s.

Strange markings were found on the bedrock several feet below the ground's surface when workers were building the bridge across the Cumberland River on Route 119. I personally know an elderly lady whose husband and brother-in-law were in the work crew that found these markings. Experts have studied the signs and are convinced they are not of Indian origin. By following the direction these symbols indicated, seven men found a small opening at the northern end of the huge cavern. Clearing away debris at this previously unknown entrance, the men entered the cave and were amazed to find a rock bridge that crossed an underground stream. Across the bridge they could see huge stone chairs and tables, along with what appeared to be stacks of large bricks. Along the walls, as far as their lights could penetrate, huge murals depicted extinct animals and large, strangely dressed people. The men swore that a large stone tree reflected their lamps' light as if it were metal. None of the men would cross the bridge. They reported their discovery to their foreman, who contacted government officials. For some unexplained reason, the officials had the cave entrance sealed immediately with tons of rock. No cause for this action was ever given local officials, but they were warned to leave the cavern closed. It remains sealed today.

Author's Note: Are the rumbling sounds and movement of the building caused by an underground stream? Is the smoke really gases from the earth's core, gases which might cause hallucinations? This would account for the inability to breathe and the sensation of being on fire that several people claim to have experienced. But why will no lights burn in this old house?

The "Old Ones"

When the first white pioneers moved into eastern Kentucky, the few Indians left in the area told a story of ghosts and campfires seen in a particular field. These apparitions are referred to in early Indian legends and are called the "old ones." The legends say drums and singing can be heard, but never refer to an apparition speaking. Many people have witnessed the phenomenon, both day and night.

In the center of this field is a perfect circle about 40 feet in diameter. The path of the circle is about a foot wide, and, although nothing will grow in this path, a strange type of grass does grow within the circle. Transplants of other grasses and weeds have been tried within the circle, but they all died in a short time. The area has been examined by agricultural experts, but they have no explanation.

Several times a year, seven campfires can be seen from a distance burning within the circle or around the edges. There have been instances when people unfamiliar with local lore thought the grass was actually burning. Many have gone out to investigate, but the fires always disappear when approached, leaving no sign of fire. During a heavy rainfall the field becomes soaked, but apparently, no rain ever falls within the circle. The air on the field is always several degrees cooler than the temperature surrounding the field. This holds true even on the hottest days. There is no perceptible breeze or wind as one steps into the field, only a feeling similar to entering a cooled room.

Birds do not build nests here, and no wild animal has ever been seen in or near this field. When dogs are led by a leash to the area, they cringe in terror and try to break away. Years ago, when the field was plowed for crops, two men were needed: one to handle the plow while another held the horses' heads to keep them from breaking away.

Strange items of flint and metal, axes, knives and other tools that appear new have been found in this field as recently as 1980. In 1900, a 60-pound granite war ax, a pair of moccasins, and a knife of tremendous size were found. The items were so huge that the person who could use them would likely have been nearly 12 feet tall. The spectral visitors left behind things unknown to the Indians of 1750-1800. Items found include metallic bows and arrows, bags, moccasins and wide belts of leather. The designs and needlework skills show a knowledge of leather art far more sophisticated than the Indians the pioneers met in the 1770s.

There are no recorded cases of these ghostly visitors harming anyone; in fact, they helped people in several instances.

An entire family was saved in 1835 by the ghostly visitors. Seven members of the family had contracted the dreaded killer, cholera. One day an Indian squaw appeared at the family's home. She motioned to one of the young men who had not yet come down with the disease, indicating that he should follow her. She led him to the woods near the house where she pointed out several plants and urged him to dig the roots. He gathered the roots the squaw had pointed out and followed her back to the house. She indicated that he was to boil the roots. After they had boiled sufficiently, she mixed a tea-like drink with a white, powdery substance she took from a leather pouch she carried around her waist. After giving a cup of the mixture to each sick member of the family, she smiled, waved farewell and left. She had never spoken a word in the presence of anyone in the family. Every sick family member recovered, but they never saw the Indian squaw again nor learned the secret of the medication.

Edward Clemons was saved by the ghostly visitors late one night in 1925. He was riding his horse within a few hundred yards of the field, when the horse bolted at the sight of the campfires and ran. Clemons explained later that he had lost control of the horse and probably would have been killed except that a huge Indian ran from the field, grabbed the horse's head and wrestled it to the ground. As he held it there, the Indian touched the horse's eyes, which immediately calmed it. The Indian picked Clemons up like a child and set him back on the horse and, with a wave, disappeared back toward the campfires.

In 1939 12-year-old Stephen Collins was swimming alone in the river about a mile from the field when cramps seized him. Because of the distance, his cries for help could not be heard by his family. Recounting the near-tragedy later, Stephen said that he was almost unconscious when a tall Indian came from nowhere, waded into the river, picked him up, carried him to shore and set him down. The Indian then waved his hand and walked away.

There was an older woman who lived alone within two miles of this field. Although there were no deer in the area, she would serve venison to her visitors. When asked where she had obtained it, she swore that two large Indians left the fresh meat on her porch several times a year.

In 1949, John Bowman, present owner of the farm, dug into three Indian graves near the site where the ghosts are seen. He removed large numbers of artifacts, some of flint, others of metal. He also found axes, knives, tools, and what were thought to be religious totems. Many of these items were beautiful works of some ancient art.

Bowman, an intelligent man, was not given to superstitions. He says that on the third night after taking the artifacts from the graves, he and his family could hear a loud, weird, moaning sound all around their house. This went on for three sleepless nights. On the fourth night, Bowman and his family were sitting on their porch when a large Indian dressed in buckskins came into the yard. Bowman owned several large, vicious dogs that began to bark and ran to attack the Indian. He waved his hand, and the dogs turned and ran, yelping in fear. They did not return home for several days.

The Indian never spoke. He pointed at Bowman; then he pointed in the direction of the disturbed graves, held up three fingers, and clapped his hands together one time. As quickly as he had appeared, he turned and started walking toward the field where he disappeared. The incident was witnessed by the entire family. Bowman immediately reburied the artifacts, and they remain buried today. The moaning sound that had kept the family awake for three nights stopped and has never been heard again. The graves are guarded against further disturbance.

The campfires can still be seen several times a year. There are times when ghostly figures can be seen moving about the circle. At other times, only the fires are seen.

It is this field where the seven campfires and Indian apparitions have been observed.

John Gillium's Revenge

John Gillium was one of the few men from Kentucky who went to Cuba in 1899 with Teddy Roosevelt's Rough Riders. About a year before he left his eastern Kentucky home for the war, Gillium had married the attractive Irene Stidham. When he left, he advised all the young men in the neighborhood to keep away from his wife while he was gone.

Gillium was killed in Cuba. There were several witnesses who saw him and his horse blown up. Only pieces of either body were ever recovered. His cavalry sword and pistol were never found.

When Joseph Larch, a young man in the community, heard about Gillium's death, he talked the young widow into letting him move in with her. Lonely, Irene agreed to the arrangement. The liaison was frowned upon by most neighbors; but the young couple caused no trouble, so the situation was tolerated.

Irene and Joseph had been living together about a year when she first saw a man who looked exactly like her dead husband. He was dressed in riding breeches, wore a campaign hat, and carried a cavalry sword and pistol. On each occasion the man would stand at the edge of the timberline on a small hill in back of the house and stare at Irene intently each time she went outside; then he would walk back into the woods. He always led a large black horse but never mounted it. He always stood on the exact spot where Irene had last seen her husband as he walked up the path and into the woods on his way to Cuba.

Several days after she first saw the stranger, Irene finally told Joseph about him. When they went to the window so she could point out the spot where the man always appeared, they saw him standing there, looking down at the house. Knowing that John Gillium was dead, and determined to learn the identity of this stranger, Joseph took his rifle, slipped out the back door and circled the hill. This positioned him behind the stranger, who was still watching the house, the large black stallion beside him.

Joseph aimed his rifle and told the man to turn around; but the man did not move, did not even seem to hear him. Joseph fired; and the man fell, turning onto his back. Joseph Larch later swore the body had no face. The black horse stood over the body and refused to let Joseph near it.

Two young boys playing in the woods had heard Joseph approach and had hidden in the bushes. They witnessed the shooting and ran home to tell their parents, who called the law. By the time Joseph returned to Irene's, the sheriff and his deputies were there, and had him accompany them to the scene of the shooting. Joseph was amazed to see that the dead man's body was face down in a large pool of blood. Again, the horse, feet planted firmly astride the man, stopped all attempts to examine the body. Tracks were evident where the horse had been walking around the body.

It was nearly dark, and not wanting to kill the animal, the men decided to wait until the next morning to retrieve the body. They hoped that during the night the horse would wander away. Joseph was arrested and taken to jail.

Returning the next morning, the sheriff and his men were amazed to find that both the dead man and the horse were gone. There was no pool of blood, no indication of horse tracks; and hours of searching failed to turn up any evidence of a shooting. It was as if the tragedy had never occurred.

The sheriff stopped by Irene's house to check on her and to see if she wanted to visit Joseph at the jail. He found her lying in bed on her back with a short cavalry saber through her stomach and a look of terror on her face. She had been dead several hours.

The sheriff returned to his office and was told that Joseph was dead also. Fingernail marks and bruises on his swollen neck clearly indicated that he had been strangled to death;

but the jailer and two deputies swore that Joseph had not been out of his cell all night and that no one had visited him. Although the coroner admitted that it was impossible for a man to choke himself to death, Joseph Larch's death was declared a suicide...there was no other logical answer.

The deaths of Irene Gillium and Joseph Larch have never been explained. Did John Gillium somehow come back from the dead to punish them? The tragedy is a matter of court record; only the names have been changed.

Author's Note: Investigation into John Gillium's military records reveal that he was definitely killed in action in Cuba by an exploding shell. At the time of his death. Gillium was wearing riding breeches, a campaign hat and, because of the rough terrain, was leading his large black horse up the hill.

Money and the Ghost
of Peter Tyler

Among these rocks is where the Civil War apparition has been seen, still guarding his money.

Between 1861 and 1865, contingents of both the Confederate and Union armies were scattered throughout the Kentucky mountains. The area was also overrun with deserters and bushwhackers. Many lives were lost in sporadic encounters. Entire families were caught up in the passion of the time...separating, fighting and dying for what they believed to be right. It was a war pitting brother against brother and breeding hatreds that, in some cases, have lasted more than 100 years. The war was also a major cause of the terrible feuds that erupted between 1890 and 1910.

One family divided by loyalties was the Tyler family. Mr. Tyler was dead and had left two sons, John and Peter, to run the family farm.

In 1862, John, the older brother, went south to join the Orphan Brigade. During some extremely heavy fighting in 1863, he was wounded, captured and sent north to a prison for the remainder of the war. Peter left his family, also in 1862, to join the Union army fighting in Virginia.

After serving for two years, he was given leave and returned home for a few days. He had been home only two days when a Northern sympathizer brought word of Rebel patrols searching farms along the North Fork of the Kentucky River, an area close to Peter's home.

It was October of 1864, and the war was not going well for the Confederacy. These Rebel patrols were looking for Union soldiers and sympathizers...not to take prisoners, but to kill.

Peter had seen many women and children made widows and orphans by the war. He had also seen too many homes burned to wait and endanger his family. Peter had about $800 in gold and silver coins. He told his wife that he planned to bury it in the rocks along the ridge in back of their house so that it would not fall into Rebel hands. He took his rifle and pack, said a hasty farewell to his wife and children, and fled up the hill, unseen by the Rebels.

It is believed that Tyler stopped long enough to bury the money under or near a large, flat rock several hundred yards up the hill directly behind his home.

Two days later, trying to reach the Ohio River and Union lines, Peter was recognized by a Southern sympathizer. A Rebel cavalry patrol was dispatched to pursue him; and since Peter was on foot, it easily overtook and captured him. The patrol took him back to the head of Miller's Branch (about three miles from his home), tied him to a tree and burned him alive. The manner of Peter's death could certainly be considered an atrocity; but emotions and fears were running high, and, in all warring armies, there are barbarous and sadistic men.

After the war was over, it was learned that Tyler had only a small amount of money with him when he was captured and killed. Both relatives and neighbors wondered what Tyler had done with the $800. Several searches were conducted by his family, but the money was never found.

Four men who had known Tyler decided to retrace his escape route in an effort to locate the hidden money. Peter Tyler's ghost was first seen when they reached the large flat rock on the ridge. They later swore that a man dressed in a blue Union uniform, with a pack and rifle, waved them away from the area. They never heard him speak, but all four saw an image they claimed looked like Tyler. During the next 50 to 60 years, the ghost was seen numerous times walking among the rocks. In the 1930s, a group of children was playing on the ridge when a man in a blue uniform yelled and chased them away. This was one of the few times the ghost was ever known to speak. The youngsters claimed that they could see through the man, and he seemed to float rather than walk. Describing what he saw, one small boy said, "He looked like smoke in the shape of a man."

The children also found $9.50 in change among the rocks—one coin a $2.50 gold piece. All the coins were dated before 1864 and believed to have been dropped by Tyler in his haste.

As late as 1978, a three-man TV crew was filming in the area, and all three swore they saw a man in a Union army uniform watching them. When they spoke to him, he disappeared. The crew deliberately tried to photograph the soldier; but when the film was developed, it showed nothing...not even a shadow.

People who have seen the ghost of the Civil War soldier believe that the ghost of Peter Tyler still guards his cache of gold and silver, even after all these years.

The Running Apparition

In southcentral Kentucky, along a well-traveled, blacktop road that leads down a steep hill to a bridge over a creek, the ghost or disembodied spirit of a young girl can sometimes be seen running, usually late at night. Persons who have witnessed this phenomenon say the girl appears suddenly, runs a short distance down the hill, but disappears before she reaches the bridge.

Years ago an old wagon road used to go down the hill, cross a ford where the bridge now stands, and continue on upstream.

A ford used to be in this stream, where the bridge is now. The ghost of a young girl has been seen running down this hill.

In 1890, a family named Chism lived on this creek several miles above the ford. When they went to and from town, they always traveled this road. As they were returning home from such a trip, the wagon tongue broke just as they started down the long steep slope. The horses ran to one side of the road while the wagon continued down the hill. Mr. and Mrs. Chism and two sons managed to leap from the wagon, but their only daughter was too frightened to jump. The vehicle careened around a short bend in the road, throwing the young girl out. Somehow she landed ahead of the wagon; and in trying to get out of the way, she rolled directly under one of the rear wheels and was killed instantly. Several years later, the young girl's ghost was seen running down the road for the first time.

This apparition has been witnessed at different times by various people, always in the same place. In one instance, a driver wrecked his truck, trying to avoid hitting what he thought was a young girl running down the hill ahead of him. Strangely, there are no screams, no sound of a rolling wagon...just the young girl running...running.

Warning in the Dust

There is a natural body and there is a spiritual body.
—I Corinthians 15:44

Virgil and Joseph Hounshell were cousins. They had been to the general store in their eastcentral Kentucky community where they bought a gallon of bootleg whiskey on that fateful night of July 7, 1937. On their way back home, they met five other young men at the mouth of Leatherwood Creek, and the seven went to a secluded spot where they played cards and drank the whiskey. An argument started, and, during the drunken brawl that followed, Virgil was fatally stabbed. Since there was no proof as to which of the men did the fatal stabbing, no one was ever tried for the crime.

Exactly one week after Virgil's death, Joseph stopped at the same store and bought some cigarettes. When he arrived home he was so scared and upset that his mother asked what was wrong. Normally, Joseph was a steady young man, but his manner was most unusual.

"I know it's impossible," Joseph said to his mother, "but I just met Virgil on the road home. At first I saw what looked like a big puff of smoke," he continued. "Then it seemed to turn into a shadow, until finally I could see Virgil, plain as day. He tried to speak, but I couldn't hear any words. Then he pointed to the ground, bent over and scratched in the dust. He wrote the numbers 7-28-37-7:30-14-D with his fingernail. He seemed to be really worried and trying awfully hard to tell me something. He stood up, shaking his head, then just seemed to turn into smoke and drift away."

Joseph told the story around the neighborhood for several days, but no one believed him. People just assumed he had been drunk, although most admitted that his story was unusual since he had seen the apparition at 3:00 in the afternoon. He also swore that he had not had a drop to drink, and his mother verified his statement.

On the night of July 28, Joseph and several other young men were again at the store drinking whiskey. Another fight started, and, during the general commotion, Joseph was stabbed twice directly in the heart. When the brawlers realized that someone was seriously hurt, the fight stopped. Two young men were tried for this murder, but, since it had been dark and over 10 people had been involved in the fight, they were not convicted.

It was on the right side of this old road that Joseph Hounshell was given a warning of his impending death by his dead cousin.

One of Joseph's brothers finally connected the earlier apparition with Joseph's death. The brother explained that 7-28-37-7:30-14-D meant: July 28, 1937 at 7:30, you have 14 days to live. The family then realized that Joseph had somehow seen his deceased cousin who had tried to warn Joseph of his own impending death.

I know this is exactly the way the strange incident happened. Joseph Hounshell was my uncle, and I knew about the numbers and the letter *D* for over a week before he was killed.

Vanishing Fire

George Washington Allen, a dishonorably discharged soldier, planned to rob two paymasters when they made their monthly visit to the Union army camp near Florence, Kentucky in September 1864. After checking their route, Allen decided the best place for the robbery would be under a large sycamore tree about a half mile from the camp. It was here the couriers always stopped to rest their horses.

Allen tied his horse out of sight a short distance away from the tree. Armed with two revolvers, he climbed the large tree to wait. When the paymasters arrived, Allen decided to kill both men first and then retrieve the money. Taking careful aim, he shot both men through their heads. Unknown to Allen, one of the couriers had saddlebags full of ammunition, and one of the bullets, after passing through the paymaster's head, struck one of these saddlebags. The resulting explosion blew the courier off his horse and enveloped him in flames. Allen also shot one of the horses. The other horse, frightened at the loud noise, ran a short distance toward the camp. In the time it took Allen to climb down the tree, catch the horse, grab the moneybags and get to his mount, soldiers from the camp were almost on the scene. Hearing the explosion, they had ridden out to investigate. Arriving and seeing the two dead couriers—one of them literally a bonfire—the soldiers spread out to see if they could find the murderer.

Allen had only gone about a mile when one of the soldiers saw him. Giving chase, the soldiers began shooting. Several bullets struck Allen and his horse, killing both. The soldiers reached Allen, but they did not find the money when they searched him. They backtracked Allen's trail, but failed to locate the missing payroll. After a fruitless investigation, the army assumed that Allen had picked out a place to hide the money and had planned to return for it later.

Several weeks later soldiers from the camp heard an explosion and saw a large fire burning under the sycamore tree. When they investigated, the fire just vanished, leaving no ashes, no burned shrubbery, no trace at all.

The explosion and fire have been heard and seen several times, along with sounds of a horse at full gallop. The galloping sound goes up to the tree and stops. Although the galloping horse and the explosion have not been heard in recent years, the fire has been seen as recently as 1981, but when approached, it disappeared without a trace.

Secret of the Rose Bush

In 1968, James Clarke left the city and moved his family to a farm in central Kentucky. It was several weeks after Clarke, his wife and their four children, and Mrs. Clarke's mother and father had moved into an abandoned farmhouse and planted most of their crops, that Clarke began to notice something strange. Each night, just as darkness began to fall, all the farm animals would stop whatever they were doing and stare down a grassy, bramble-grown path that led to an old, neglected cemetery. The cemetery was located above a long, wide meadow several hundred yards behind the barn, and the animals seemed to watch something along the path. After their eyes moved slowly along the path and reached the house...they looked away and resumed their normal activity.

Clarke watched this strange behavior for several evenings, then sought out a neighbor to ask him what he thought about the animals' unusual actions. The neighbor said that he had only one possible explanation.

A previous owner, just before his death, had vowed that he would come back to get a large amount of money buried on the property. The dying man's promise was one reason the farm had been abandoned for so long, even though no one had ever seen any type of manifestation. Several families had moved away because of the strange actions of their livestock. Some had lived there several months; others had lasted only a few days. In one instance, a large, vicious dog chased something down the path when, suddenly, he was lifted into the air, and his spine was broken in several places by something invisible. The owner and his wife witnessed this and moved away the next morning. On another occasion near dark, five people saw a large, ill-tempered bull start to chase something near the cemetery. After running in a large circle for a few minutes, the bull seemed to run into an invisible wall. His body was lifted and thrown several feet, and when he landed, his neck was broken.

Clarke was afraid to tell his family what the neighbor had said about the strange happenings; but that evening, as all of them sat on the front porch, they saw a man coming up the old path. He kept looking down at the ground as if searching for something. The man made no noise when he walked...his body seemed to glide along just above the ground.

In the near darkness Clarke thought it might be the neighbor he had talked to earlier and spoke to the man. There was no answer...whoever it was didn't even look up. It was as if he had not heard Clarke speak.

The silent stranger walked across the yard to a corner of the house and pointed his hand downward to a spot beside a large and very old rose bush. Then he turned and walked back to the old path. As he started down the slope below the cemetery, again it seemed that he floated along like smoke. When he reached the bottom, he disappeared into thin air, as though the meadow had swallowed him.

The family sat awestruck until Clarke finally regained his composure and remembered what his neighbor had said about a previous owner having buried a lot of money on the farm. He told two of his sons to get a lantern and a shovel and, accompanied by the entire family, went to the spot where the man had pointed. When they had dug down about two feet, the shovel struck metal, and Clarke brought up an old iron pot. They removed the lid and were amazed to see that the pot was almost full of gold and silver coins.

From the time the Clarke family found the valuable pot, nothing unusual was seen again. The livestock stopped being nervous at dusk and no longer watched the old path which led to the meadow.

Grisly Truth of the Haunted Bridge

A young farm couple were the first people to become aware that a large covered bridge in northeastern Kentucky was something more than ordinary. The year was 1890 and the month was July.

The young wife said that she first noticed the silence at a time of the year when creek frogs, insects and whippoorwills normally fill the air with sound. As the couple approached the halfway point across the bridge, they saw a light rise up from nowhere at the far end. At the same time, they could hear the voices of crying children. Thinking someone was hurt, the couple hurried their horse-drawn wagon toward the light and sounds. Reaching the end of the bridge, they stopped their wagon, but could see no one. The strange light was still there, and it started bobbing up and down. Seven times it bobbed; then it disappeared. After a few minutes, the light reappeared...bobbed seven times and vanished again. This sequence continued for nearly an hour. Each time, the bobbing light was accompanied by the sound of crying children. The young couple were mystified, as they were unable to locate the source for either the light or the sounds. Finally, they gave up and drove on home. They did not tell of their strange experience until several years later.

One night, in 1895, Morgan Rogers and his three sons were fishing near the covered bridge when they heard the sound of an object being dropped into the water. They heard it seven times; then it stopped a few minutes, only to start again and repeat itself. At the same time, they saw a round ball of light bob up and down seven times at the end of the bridge. They did not hear the crying children as others had done.

The mysterious lights on the bridge caused a tragedy in 1900. Frank Hardin, he wife and young baby were crossing the bridge in a wagon when the light bobbed up in front of their team. The horses, terrified, bolted so quickly that Frank could not control them. As they careened off the bridge, the wagon struck a rock and overturned, killing Hardin's wife and baby. Hardin left the county after the accident.

For the next 20 years, the bobbing light and strange sounds were seen and heard frequently, and the structure became known as the "haunted bridge." The county built a new road which bypassed the bridge, and the old road was abandoned.

In 1925, during a severe summer electrical storm, hikers sought shelter under the abandoned bridge. The hikers thought they were safe, but lightning struck the bridge, killing two of them and setting the bridge on fire. Braving the fire, the remaining hikers dragged out the two bodies, then went to the county seat and reported the incident to the sheriff's office.

Half of the bridge was destroyed by the fire, and county authorities decided to finish the demolition. Wreckers, reaching the end of the bridge where the mysterious lights had been seen and crying had been heard, found that one of the four wooden beams supporting the sides and roof of the bridge was hollow. When they looked inside, they found the skeletons of seven small children. Each child had a small round hole in its skull, proof that each had been killed. An investigation was conducted by the sheriff's department. Old records revealed that there had been a migrant camp for farm and sawmill workers located on the river a short distance from the covered bridge from 1840 to 1885. It was suspected, but never proven, that an itinerant worker had killed the children and hidden the bodies in the hollow bridge timbers. Records also revealed that during that same period, over 25 small children had disappeared throughout the county. The authorities never investigated or tied the disappearances together since they were widely separated in area and had covered a period of 45 years. The identities of the children were never known since the remains could not be identified. Later, however, they were given Christian burials in the local cemetery. Who killed the children and put their bodies in the hollow beam remains a mystery.

After the skeletons were found and the bridge was destroyed, the bobbing light and crying children were never seen or heard again.

Five Legends of Wilderness Road

In southeastern Kentucky there is an area barely three square miles in size which is home to five separate and distinct ghost stories. The blacktopped road which leads into the area follows a part of the old Wilderness Road, famous in Kentucky history. The unexplained phenomena occur along a large stream that intersects this road.

One of the stories had its origin more than 100 years ago. Through the years there have been reports of things unseen which follow people...even touching some of them. Travellers on foot related incidents of hearing footsteps walking beside them. Some have said they not only heard the footsteps, but also felt the touch of a hand on their shoulder or neck, even though nothing was in sight. Horseback riders have told of something unseen that jumped on their horses with them. Some have said they even felt arms around their waists after the invisible haunt joined the rider. There have also been reports that the sudden advent of the obscure wraith occasionally frightened horses to such an extent that they bolted with their riders and ran out of control for miles. This particular spirit is not known to have ever bothered anyone in a road wagon, but seemed to develop a particular affinity for cars as they gradually replaced wagons. Folks driving automobiles along this lonely stretch of road have reported many involvements. Several have related incidents when something heavy either jumped or fell on top of their car or on the car's hood. Sometimes there was more than just loud sound. The hood of the car was actually bent from the weight of the object, even though no fallen rock, tree limbs or other such objects were ever found. One driver said he hit something in the road. He had seen nothing, but got out to investigate in case he had accidentally hit a person or an animal. He searched carefully but could find nothing that he might have hit. The only confirmation that there had been something was the smashed grill on his automobile.

In this area there are several small coal mines where local people get coal for use in their homes. There have been several reports by folks who say they have seen lights inside these mines at night when they know there is no one there. Several of these folks claim to have seem a woman and sometimes a small boy inside some of these mines. The two are always reported to be dressed in white, and when approached by anyone, they simply disappear.

Close by a stream and near this old road is an area several hundred feet square, where cool air can be felt all year. It's like entering an air-conditioned room when a certain invisible line is crossed. It is a favorite spot for local children to play. Several children in the neighborhood told me that sometimes they feel cool air blowing down on the backs of their necks. This eliminates my theory that the cool air comes from a crevice, or possibly an underground cavern, in the rocks. I was there in July 1981...I didn't feel any kind of breeze, but the temperature in that spot was at least 20 degrees lower than in the area around it. Several local adults have witnessed this phenomenon, but none can explain it.

And another oddity is that, no matter where the youngsters leave their toys, or build small rock houses, or put blankets on the ground, the objects are always in a different place when they return.

A fourth observed phenomenon is a light that can be seen moving along the road for several hundred yards. The light turns off the road, into the timber, and always stops near a large rock overhang, where it stays a few minutes, then disappears. There are reports that this repeats itself several times in a given night.

The fifth happening in this area is the scream of a panther, or mountain lion. No such cats have been seen in Kentucky for over 150 years, yet this sound has scared hunters, hikers and other travelers within the last 50 years. The screaming is not of a wild domestic cat or horned own—the sounds have been taped and positively identified as being that of a mountain lion. The screaming continues, but no animal tracks or any other indication of a large cat have ever been found.

The Strange Execution of Simon Brown

Simon Brown owned many slaves. He also owned several hundred acres of rich bottomland, which these slaves worked during the 20 years preceding the Civil War. Brown was a cruel and arrogant man with no compassion for anyone. He considered slaves as animals, to be bred and worked like animals, for his own personal gain. He was not a religious man and lived only for himself.

According to family records, Brown was given three distinct and emphatic warnings to change his ways...

The first occurred in 1848. A slave had not cared for Brown's horse as instructed, so Brown ordered the slave be put in a large kettle out in a field under the sun. Brown posted an armed guard with orders that the Negro was not, under any circumstances, to get out. As further torture, the pot, normally used as a boiler for making maple syrup, was placed near the river so that the slave could see water he could not drink. After five days in the kettle without food or water, the Negro died. Brown had him buried and promptly forgot the incident. This was only one of many slaves that Brown had killed over several years.

Three nights later, Simon Brown awoke from a sound sleep to see the pale figure of a Negro slave standing near the bedroom window. His arms were outstretched in a pleading gesture; his face was contorted in pain. The apparition pointed down several times then seemed to evaporate. Brown's wife also saw it.

The second warning came two years later, in 1850. Brown had split up several of the slave families he owned, selling some members to a plantation owner in Mississippi. The blacks begged to remain together, but their entreaties meant nothing to Brown...the new owner had paid a high price for them, and profit was all Brown wanted. It was learned later that two of the elderly slaves had died on the way to Mississippi.

Three nights after Brown committed this atrocity, he received another warning. Brown and three other landowners were returning home from a nearby town when the apparition of several slaves appeared in the road. The horses became frightened, but one of the ghosts reached up and touched the team, and the animals calmed down immediately. Three of the figures pointed directly at Brown then down toward the ground. The gesture was repeated three times, then the figures disappeared. One of Brown's companions told him, "You had better start treating your slaves a little better. This is your second warning." (Simon had told two of the men about his previous experience, so they saw this as the threat it turned out to be.)

Instead of showing compassion, Brown's treatment of his slaves became even more brutal. He cut their food supply in half, working hours were increased, and Brown used his blacksnake whip at the slightest provocation. The inhumane treatment was the talk of the neighborhood, and his acquaintances began to avoid him. Everything seemed to intensify his cruelty toward both his slaves and his neighbors.

The third and final warning came after Brown ordered a slave thrown into the fireplace used to heat the parlor and large hall of the mansion. The unfortunate Negro was tied to one of the six-foot logs that the fireplace accommodated, and two other slaves were forced to throw him to the back of the fire where the heat was most intense. He died a painful death.

Several nights later, Brown, his wife, two children and a trusted servant were on their way to a nearby town when they began to hear a low moaning sound. As the unearthly noise continued, shadowy figures began to emerge along the road until finally, a line of figures stood in the road. (For some reason, this time the team of horses did not become frightened.)

Each of the ghosts held up one hand, three fingers extended, but this time they did not point to the ground. The figures stood in the road for a few minutes, then seemed to blow away like smoke. Brown's wife and children were terrified, but he assured them that the slaves were trying to trick them.

After this frightful sighting, the news that Brown had burned a slave reached the neighborhood. A committee of 15 men formed to talk to Simon Brown, not on behalf of the slaves, but because of concern for the reputation of the community. (Legally, the committee could do nothing about Brown's treatment of his slaves. Slaves were considered personal property to be handled in any manner their owner thought best.) The 15 men drove to Brown's farm in three buggies. Just before reaching the huge mansion, they saw Simon Brown standing in a large, open, snow-covered field. Brown was wearing no coat or boots; he appeared to be looking at something that the men could not see. The scene was so unusual that the men stopped.

Suddenly, Brown started to run, but he seemed to be caught by invisible hands. The men watched from their buggies as Brown was thrown to the ground. They could hear the sounds of whips and the clanking of metal above the terrible screams. Within a few minutes, Brown lay still, alone in the snowy field which was now completely quiet.

The men approached the body and were amazed to see that it had been burned in several places. There was an iron slave collar around his neck, thumb screws (used to control slaves) were on his hands, and leg irons were on his feet. What was left of Simon Brown's face was contorted in a look of horror, the likes of which the man had never seen. There were no footprints except Brown's, no signs of a struggle, no tools or whips...nothing but the undisturbed snow and the manacled, mutilated body of Simon Brown.

It was daylight, clear weather—all those men could not have been mistaken in what they saw happen.

There were 15 witnesses present at the death of Simon Brown, and there were witnesses at each of the apparent warnings, but questions remain unanswered. Perhaps the most incredible of the mysteries is: who or what could have induced Brown to go barefoot and without a coat into an open field that was covered with snow? His wife thought he was in the upstairs bedroom sleeping. Why was he walking, on a day of below freezing temperatures, when he normally rode a horse? How did he get into the field without leaving tracks that the neighbors could see?

People in the area say that the screams of the slave who died in the big iron kettle can still be heard sometimes along the strip of bottomland. But, late at night, when the mist rises from the river, when one uses a little imagination, almost anything can be heard or seen.

PART II
Unexplained Phenomena

The Vanishing Bird Family

About 1900, a family, considered to be very strange by their few, isolated neighbors, lived on a high point above the North Fork of the Kentucky River. There were nine members in this family, and they lived in a large log house built in an unusual oblong fashion. They made no friends and allowed no one except the family to enter their home.

On occasion, people passing along the road in front of this dwelling could hear screams and a flapping sound such as a large-winged bird might make. There were also sounds of high-pitched voices and the sound of blows such as might be made if a person were being beaten. At night passersby in Williams Creek might hear a splash as if a large object were being dropped into the water. The sound was always heard near this house. No one ever saw any lights at night, and no smoke was ever seen coming from the chimney. Eventually, the sounds from this house became the talk of the few families living upstream.

Years passed, and a graveyard appeared on the hill behind the house, although no neighbors had ever heard of a death or burial in the family. Several years after it was first noticed, the graveyard had grown to contain over 50 small tombstones made of plain creek rock. Strangely, it appeared there were still nine members in the family. They were seen separately, at various times, in the local village some two miles away, where they purchased only bare necessities, but they always bought some type of grain.

Not only did they appear to be the same individuals, but they seemed never to grow any older. They were physically small, and the few people who ever saw them up close swore their faces resembled those of birds, with long noses and receding chins. They all walked with a quick, jerky kind of step, spoke in high-pitched voices, and always wore gloves and long coats.

After about 10 years, curiosity got the best of a group of men, and they made plans to check on the actions of this strange family. They wanted some explanations...how did they live—they did very little farming and owned no farm animals...why did they seem never to age...why did a cemetery continue to grow when there were no known deaths in the family? Before going to talk to the odd family, though, the men checked on travellers who were known to have used the road. They found no reports of missing persons, violence or death.

On a clear, moonlit night, about 50 men assembled to visit the unusual family. They formed two groups so they could approach the house from different directions. One group reached the front yard as the other came into the back yard, and all were amazed to see nine large birds fly away from the rooftop of the house. They entered the large dwelling to find nothing but piles of straw resembling huge birds' nests. No furniture, clothes, tools or other human necessities were found.

The next morning the men investigated the graveyard. They opened some 20 of the graves and found small human skeletons. The skeletons revealed an amazing trait never before seen by any of those present. Each had two large extra bones along the shoulder. This seemed to indicate that while the bodies appeared human, they had somehow developed the ability to fly. The bones were hollow, like those of birds, and some of the first bodies to be buried had completely disintegrated. Before leaving, the men burned the house, and the area was avoided after that.

What kind of creatures were these? Where had they come from; where did they go? The number of graves would indicate an impossible birth rate for a normal, human family. Might the sounds of objects being dropped into the large creek have been eggs that would not hatch? (A bird will throw these out of the nest, especially one without a shell.) All traces of the house's foundation, the cemetery and the bridge are gone now, and only slight indentations above the river show where the old road used to be.

Today, on the high point of land where the dwelling stood, some unusual blackbirds are occasionally seen. They are exceptionally large and seem reluctant to fly away. They watch and follow people who come near. At times it seems they are trying to speak.

Author's Note: My grandmother, born in 1877, heard this story firsthand from neighbors who were among the men who exhumed the bodies of the "bird people" and helped burn the house. She and other elderly persons told me the story when I was about 15 years old.

Tragedy at Devil's Hollow

Author found this old gun, of the period 1865-1880 that could have belonged to one of the Callahans or Deatons.

James Steven Taylor and Charles Edward Davis were out of college for the summer. It was July 1961, and the two young Lexington men had never been into the real Kentucky mountains. For that reason they decided to make the trip into the deep Appalachians for a few days of serious camping and fishing.

After driving the better part of three hours, they came to

the little mountain town of Hypen, stopping their Jeep at the first service station.

"Where's a good place around here to camp and do some fishing?" James asked the station attendant.

Several men, loafing around the station, eased up from their seats to admire the new four-wheel-drive Jeep the boys were driving. The gathering included Deputy Sheriff William Clark and State Trooper John Combs. Everyone there seemed to have a different piece of advice to offer about the best fishing holes.

"Don't pay any attention to that bunch of loafers," the attendant joked. "They're too lazy to fish! If you want some real good fishing, head on over to the Middle Fork of Kentucky River. Several folks have been landing some real good ones over there."

Middle Fork sounded good to James and Charles, so they asked the attendant for directions. He explained that they would need to take County Road 28 through the gap in the mountains. He pointed out the ridge about two miles away.

"When you get through the gap, turn right on the first gravel road," he continued. "That gravel road will take you down Devil's Holler to Middle Fork."

By the time the Jeep was filled with gas, and the two young men had bought some extra bait, it was getting on toward dark. The boys thanked the attendant for his help and drove off in the direction of Devil's Hollow and Middle Fork.

As they approached the gap in the crest of the mountain, Charles pointed out what appeared to be a blanket of fog hanging over the road ahead. Both agreed that conditions weren't right for fog, and all else around the area appeared bright and clear. Even though they were mystified, they drove on into the smoke-like mist. It seemed to take only seconds before they were in the clear again, and the fog had vanished as if it had never been there. Immediately, they noticed a change in the air. It smelled fresher and cleaner.

Following their instructions, the two vacationers turned right on the first gravel road and started down the hill to Devil's Hollow. James was the first to notice a change in the road and the surroundings.

"Charles, have you noticed how much lighter it is now?" James asked. "It was almost dark when we left that little town back there. This road sure is different, too. There has never been any gravel on this trail!"

"Let's pull up here a minute," Charles suggested. "Let's get out that topographic map that you brought. We must have made a wrong turn somewhere. This road looks like a car has never been along here. These ruts look more like they were made by old road wagons."

They pulled to a stop and got out the map. To their amazement, they could find no road such as the one they were on.

"Charles, there's definitely something wrong here," James exclaimed. "Just look at the trees! This forest has never been touched by loggers. Somewhere I read that all of Kentucky was logged over in the 1900s. And that stream over there.... It appears to be a lot larger than the one shown on this map."

As the boys looked up and down the valley, they saw a large log building, which they decided might have been a country store. With all these unexpected surroundings, the young vacationers decided they had best find someone and ask where they were.

As they neared the log building, they saw several back-woodsy types lounging on the porch. Most of them wore full beard and eyed the approaching strangers with suspicion. They seemed especially in awe of the Jeep. One or two appeared about ready to run, and several horses hitched nearby did break loose and gallop away.

The boys couldn't help but wonder if they had stumbled onto a location for an 1870s motion picture. On the other hand, if such were the case, there would be cameras and other equipment...including trucks and trailers. By the same token, the men and horses would not be frightened by the approach of one little Jeep.

"I have a feeling we've stumbled onto something that's even stranger than it looks," James said.

One of the tall, bearded men, dressed in overalls, a denim

shirt and a pair of boots, stepped out from the porch and approached James and Charles. A pair of large revolvers were strapped around his waist.

"You'uns air on my land," the man said in a voice that boomed with authority. "Who air ye, and what do ye want?"

"We seem to be lost," Charles said as calmly as the shaky circumstances would allow. "I guess we made a wrong turn when we came through that fog back up there at the gap. I'm Charles Davis, and this is James Taylor. We're from Lexington, and we came down here to camp and do a little fishing."

"What kind of a contraption is that ye're ridin' in?" the bearded one continued. "I ain't never seed a wagon like that afore. Whar's yer hosses? What pulls hit?"

The young men from Lexington set about trying to explain that the vehicle they were driving was a Jeep and that it didn't need horses to pull it. No matter how they put it, their audience didn't seem to understand or believe much of what they were told.

"Hit don't make no sense atall," the two-gun spokesman decided. "Never heered of sech a thing. And besides, there ain't no fog 'round hyar this time of yar.

"Ye wouldn't be Deatons, would ye?" he continued suspiciously. "Cause ifen ye air, ye shore made a bad mistake comin' through thet gap. Just in case ye don't know, I be Devil Joe Callahan. These fellers hyar be kinfolks, and we aim to kill ever' low-down Deaton that lives."

"Honest, we're not Deatons, and neither of us are kin to any Deatons," Charles pleaded. "My name is Charles Davis, and my friend is James Taylor. Both of us are from Lexington."

The two young men explained that they were attending college in Lexington and were out of school for the summer. They had come to this part of the state for some camping and fishing. They reviewed how they had stopped in the little town of Hypen, just over the ridge, and asked for advice on where they might go for some good fishing. They told the Callahans that a service station attendant had told them to come through the gap and turn right on the first gravel road.

After explaining how they came to be in their present location and their puzzlement about the abrupt change in the road, Davis and Taylor asked Callahan if the group of men at the store were dressed up as a promotion for some community celebration...reasoning that it was unusual to see so many dressed in that fashion in 1961.

"Whut do ye mean, 1961?" Callahan asked angrily. "Anybody knows the yar is 1879, and we don't dress no different than nobody else."

The boys could see they had made a mistake in the way they spoke about the clothes the men were wearing. They hastened to explain that they meant no harm.

"Best watch yer tongue," Callahan warned them. "I got lotsa enemies, and I don't take no chances with strangers. A smart mouth can get ye in a heap of trouble.

"Come on with me down to my cabin," the tall mountaineer continued. "I want to talk to ye. Both of ye keep yer hands where they can be seed."

Without waiting for an answer, Devil Joe turned on his heel and started down the creek. Charles and James exchanged worried glances, but they had no choice other than to follow the tall clan leader. Leaving the Jeep behind, they walked the few hundred yards to his cabin.

Several hounds lay in the shade of trees that surrounded the house. Chickens clucked around the yard, and several pigs rooted under the porch. A garden patch was located on one side of the cabin. Curious children peered around corners and from behind curtains at the two strangely dressed men.

"Set a spell," boomed Devil Joe. "That tale ye told me don't make no sense atall, and I fer sure don't understand what ye be doin' here, but I aim to find out! Don't worry none. Ye won't be kilt lessen I give the word. Ye ain't a-packin' no pistols, air ye? If ye air, bring 'em out slow 'cause they's two rifles a-pintin' at ye from across the holler yander. And them fellers don't miss what they shoot at."

"We don't have any guns, Mr. Callahan, and we're sure not

looking for any trouble," James assured him.

"Thet be good," Devil Joe replied. "I'll take your word thet ye ain't got no guns. Jist remember all hit takes is a wave of muh hand and ye're dead. Now, tell me, what's all this fool-ishness about 1961 ye been talkin' about?"

"We can't understand it either, but it's the honest truth! When we left Hypen it was July 12, 1961, and almost dark," Charles explained. "Somehow, we ended up here in the early afternoon, and you tell us the year is 1879."

"Son, this is July, right enough, and fer shore hit's 1879," Devil Joe replied. "I jist can't figure out where ye come from er how ye got hyar."

"Something must have happened to us when we came through the fog at the gap," James commented. "All we came down here for was to camp for a few days and do some fishing."

"Son, thet's hard fer me to believe," Callahan mused. "I got to admit I ain't seed no clothes like the two of ye air wear-ing. And that wagon ye call a Jeep...ain't never seed nothing like hit! Now, I have heard of people disappearin'. Over in Jessee County a whole family went to bed one night and warn't never seed agin. The house, the barns and livestock wuz gone, and the next day bushes wuz a-growin' where the farm had been! Damnedest thing I ever seed!

"Want a drink of 'shine?" Devil Joe changed abruptly. Without waiting for an answer, he turned and shouted over his shoulder, "Hey, Luke, fetch a jug out hyar, we'uns got company!"

From somewhere inside the cabin the sounds of a rifle butt striking the floor and the clinking of jugs were heard. In a matter of moments a younger image of Devil Joe Callahan emerged from a doorway carrying a jug of clear liquid.

"This hyar's Luke, one of my boys," Devil Joe said. "I had 10 boys 'til them Deatons kilt four of 'em."

Devil Joe went on to explain that two of his boys, Clyde and Ed, were married and that Jamie, Billy and Phil were still single and living at home. He said that he had two daughters, Ruth and Pearl, both married and living in Ohio.

"The Deatons tied three of my boys to trees and shot 'em like dogs. The fourth one they bushwhacked down clost to the mouth of this hyar holler." Callahan grimaced as he recalled the events. "We'uns been a-fightin' them Deatons more'n five yars now. Ye can see why I don't trust strangers."

Something about the two young strangers seemed to impress Devil Joe. He offered them a drink from the jug Luke had brought and watched each of them keenly as he took a swig. His judgment of men had saved his life more than once. He had heeded his premonitions for too many years to ignore them now. While these two young strangers talked funny and dressed funny, there was something about them that led him to believe that they were telling him the truth.

"Thet horseless wagon up by the store might be hard to explain to folks," Devil Joe thought out loud. "They be folks around hyar thet still believe in witches, ghosts and sich things. Course, I don't take no stock in nothin' like thet myself. I believe a 69-caliber rifle ball will kill any livin' thing ifen ye hit it right."

"You'uns jist stay with us fer a spell. Maybe we can figger out how ye got hyar. Ye can fish down to the river. Ain't more'n three mile from hyar. I'd be obliged ifen ye'd tell me more about whar ye're from."

Charles and James looked at each other and nodded agreement.

"This could be just the place we're looking for," Charles suggested. "Peace and quiet, along with some good fishing."

Callahan warned them that things might not always be so quiet or peaceful if the Deatons should come around.

"We would sure like to stay awhile, Mr. Callahan," James replied. "There are a good many questions that I would like to ask you."

Callahan still had some questions of his own that he wanted to clear up in his mind. He asked them again about the fog which the boys said they had come through at the gap.

"I recollect some mighty onnatural things that happened in the war. All thet us fellers from the South wuz a-doin' wuz protectin' our own. Them damn Yankees wuz the cause of it all, a-tryin' to tell us how to live. Hit were in 1861, I wuz a-livin' in Alabam when we got word thet the Yankees wuz agonna take the slaves away from us. Well, thet were a mistake. Them slaves wuz our tools! Without 'em cotton couldn't be growed!"

The mountain man went on to tell the boys how he had moved to his present home along with his wife and nine children. They bought their farm and started a little store. The two youngest boys were born after they moved to Kentucky.

"I reckon things would be good ifen it warn't fer this damn feud with them Deatons," Callahan said.

Turning again to his Civil War experiences, Callahan related a bizarre event he witnessed while serving in South Carolina.

"We wuz a-tryin' to take a bridge them Yankees wuz a-guardin'. As we charged their breastworks, a bunch of soljers dressed in knee britches, blue coats and three-cornered hats come acrost thet bridge. We charged right through 'em. We could see 'em, but we couldn't feel nuthin'. I tell ye, it beat all I'd ever seed!"

Callahan went on to tell the boys how his outfit took the bridge and some Yankee prisoners, too. He said the Yankees were scared half to death when they saw the soldiers in blue coats. One of the Yankee officers said the blue coats were ghosts from the Revolutionary War.

"I don't know whut they wuz, but I still don't believe in no ghosts nor witches."

Devil Joe continued his strange tales from the war. He recalled that once when they were fighting in Tennessee something like a big bird flew over the battlefield. He said that while it looked like a bird, it didn't flap its wings, left a trail of smoke behind it and made an awfully loud noise. He said it circled the battlefield a few times and then flew away.

He recalled an occasion in Virginia when a group of Confederate soldiers were charging a hill being held by Yankees. The soldiers charged up the hill into a patch of fog. They went into the fog, but they never came out again.

"I don't talk much about the war," Callahan said. "They wuz a bunch of strange things thet happened, and a lot of killin' wuz done fer nuthin', the way I see hit."

Because of his own strange encounters or because of something in the boys' appearance, Devil Joe Callahan had cast aside his usual mistrust of strangers and decided that he and his family could safely accept them in their midst.

"Ye fellers air welcome to stay hyar long's ye like," he told them. "We got plenty room. You'uns can sleep in the loft."

With Luke Callahan as a guide and companion, James and Charles left the cabin early the next morning and spent the day fishing. For the next two days they hunted squirrel with Devil Joe. The two young men were developing a strong liking and a growing admiration for this tall mountaineer.

After a few days, Charles became despondent. Reality had overtaken him, and he began to realize that they really were back in the year 1879. As they sat on the river bank fishing, Charles said, "James, I'm worried. We've been here a week now. I'm beginning to wonder if we will ever get back home and to our own time. I sure wish there was a way to get back to 1961. You know that wagon road we came in on? I wonder where it leads to."

James related how Devil Joe had told him earlier that the wagon road through the gap went on to Hypen.

"The road would be rough, but I'm sure we could get the Jeep through the gap," James continued. "For some reason, though, I don't think we should try to go into town just yet.

"We've been lucky, Charles," he continued. "Devil Joe and his family like us in spite of the fact that they can't understand how we got here. Maybe we'll turn up a clue soon that will help us solve the question of how we go about getting back to 1961. Do we just drive on out and try to force a reversal of whatever process got us here...or will whatever brought us here take us back in its own good time?

"Perhaps we should just be patient and go on with our fishing and hunting. After all, who from our time ever had the opportunity to enjoy this part of the state as it was 80 years ago?"

"I'll have to admit this has been the best vacation I've ever had," Charles replied. "Devil Joe sure isn't like the old mountaineers I've read about. But I do wish we could let our parents know. It sure seems strange: no phones, no cars, no television, no radio, no ice cream or newspapers. You don't think we'll have to stay here in 1879, do you?"

James reassured Charles by telling him that there was sure to be a way out of their predicament.

"Tonight, we'll talk some more with Devil Joe," James went on. "He seems to have encountered a lot of strange things. Maybe our talk with him will turn up something that might help us."

After supper that evening the Callahans and their visitors from another time gathered on the porch to relax and talk awhile before bedtime.

"Mr. Callahan," Charles opened the conversation, "we've really enjoyed the last few days. We don't understand how we got here, but getting to know you and your family has been something mighty special for us."

Devil Joe assured them that the Callahans were glad to have them. Not only was he pleased that they were there, but he was especially pleased that there had been no trouble from the Deatons during their stay.

"I'm obliged to ye fellers fer tellin' about the things ye say be true 80 yars from now," the bearded patriarch continued. "I don't see how ye could've lived in thet time and come back to this'un, but I've seed enough strange things thet I won't say hit can't be. I ain't a-doubtin' yer word, but hit shore is peculiar. Imagine, lights thet burn without no oil, a box with pictures that move and talk. How in hell can ye talk into a box and speak with somebody miles away that ye can't even see? And all thet noise from them horseless wagons ye talk about would surely be enough to drive a person crazy. Hit would be somethin' to see, though, wouldn't hit, Betty?"

"Joe," Mrs. Callahan spoke up, "ye remember that thing we saw over there across the creek several yar back? Ye know, when we'uns saw that round thing land over there at the mouth of thet holler."

"By damn, thet air right! I had plumb forgot about hit. Boys, thet were the damnedest thing we ever did see. This round thing, hit looked somethin' like a hat, come down and lit jist like a bird. Hit had four legs and didn't make a sound. They wuz lights inside of it, and they wuz flashin' off and on. We wuz out there hoein' corn when the thing lit. We wuz no more'n 15 or 20 yards from hit. Four skinny little fellers got out of thet thing. They wore clothes thet looked like shiny metal...like the inside of a gun barrel. They come down to the creek, took some water and a few rocks, then went right back.

"Jamie, Luke and Billy run back to the cabin and fetched guns, but I wouldn't let 'em shoot them little fellers. Hit didn't peer like they even seed us. I guess they wuz a-talkin' to one another, but hit sounded more like mice a-squeekin' than people a-talkin'. When they got back in thet round thing hit went right straight up. Real fast, too, and we never seed hit again."

Charles explained to Devil Joe that people were still seeing things like that in 1961...things they called flying saucers or Unidentified Flying Objects.

"I don't know whut it wuz," Joe answered, "but hit shore were a sight to see."

At this point, Devil Joe stifled a yawn and said that it was his bedtime. He went inside the cabin, promising the boys that he would show them his still tomorrow.

On the tenth day of their stay, James was joined by Luke and two of Devil Joe's small grandchildren for an afternoon of swimming and fishing. After the evening meal the entire family again gathered on the porch to talk and relax. Along with James and Charles were Devil Joe and Mrs. Callahan, Jamie, Billy, Phil, their two visiting sons, Clyde and Ed, along with their wives, three grandchildren and three nephews.

After considerable small talk about the day of fishing and swimming experienced by James, Luke and the two children, Devil Joe injected a more sobering thought.

"Shore is a mighty purty night," he began, "but they's something too quiet about hit. I got a feelin' somethin' bad's gonna happen."

The elder Callahan talked of the first meeting between himself and the young men from Lexington. He said that it was a blessing that he happened to be there when the first contact was made. He noted that a good many folks would have shot first and then concerned themselves with finding out who the boys were.

"Hit ain't often I say this about folks I ain't knowed any longer than I've knowed ye," Devil Joe continued, "but I like ye young fellers. And I'm agonna tell ye why this killin's been goin' on twixt us and them Deatons. Most times I'd jist say hit ain't nobody's business, but I want ye to know how this feud got started. We'uns been havin' trouble fer over five yars now. Like a lot of things, hit started over most nothin. I wisht hit hadn't, but hit's too late now."

Callahan related that the incident which started the trouble began one day when it was coming down a heavy rain. The creek was rising, and one of the Callahans had refused to take a boat across the creek to one of the Deatons. This made Deaton mad, and his family quit speaking to the Callahans. One day three of the Deaton boys had caught Luke and Tom Callahan on the road and beat up on them. To get even, Luke had gone back to the house, got a gun and shot one of the Deaton boys in the leg.

"Wal, later on some of them Deatons waylaid muh boy Dave down near the mouth of the holler, and they kilt him," Devil Joe explained. "I took the rest of muh boys and went acrost the ridge to Big John Deaton's place. We knowed fer shore hit were his boys what shot Dave, but we couldn't prove hit. I tried a-talkin' to John, but hit didn't do no good. I wanted to keep our families outten hit. I offered to meet him on top of the ridge at midnight with a pistol in one hand and a lantern in t'other so's jist the two of us could settle hit afore hit went too fer. But, he wouldn't do hit."

Callahan went on to recite that matters were exasperating for a time afterward. The Deatons would sneak along the ridge and run off the Callahans' cattle. Sometimes they would find a steer that had been shot. On one occasion their barn was burned in the night.

This foolishness went on for a year or two. Again, Devil Joe went to talk with John Deaton, but Deaton claimed that the Callahans had started the trouble in the first place and wouldn't listen to any overtures for a peaceful settlement.

"About two yars ago, I sent three of muh boys over on Big Troublesome Creek to buy some corn," Callahan went on. "Wal, they runned into seven of them Deatons. They all started a-quarrelin'. One word led to another and finally, somebody pulled a pistol. Two Deatons wuz kilt. The five that wuz left took muh three boys, Earl, Tom and Orville, tied 'em to trees and shot 'em to death.

"When I heered about the killin' and went to cut muh boys down and bring 'em home fer buryin', I swore a blood oath to kill every Deaton that crost muh path as long as I lived."

Devil Joe went on the relate that soon after his sons were buried, he, along with his remaining sons and some other kinfolks, sneaked over to Big John Deaton's cabin and opened fire with rifles and pistols. He said that several Deatons were killed but that he didn't know exactly how many.

He said there had been several fights between the Callahans and Deatons since then. In the ensuing time he said he had lost a brother...one who had moved there from Alabama after Devil Joe's family had arrived...and three cousins, in addition to the four sons.

"Thet's why we'uns stick purty clost together." Joe said. "Big John swears that some night he's a-gonna come over here, burn us out and kill all us Callahans. Thet's why we keep all them guns ready."

He got to his feet, told his family and the two visitors that it was bedtime and turned toward the door. As he turned, the sound of a calling bird could be heard from the distant ridge. Callahan stopped in his tracks.

"Heer thet?" he asked in a low voice. "That ain't no bird call, hit's them Deatons signalling one another. Birds like thet don't sing at night."

Quickly, he instructed his sons to have their guns and

ammunition ready, to bolt all the doors and close all the window shutters.

"I guess Big John and the Deatons air a-comin' to burn us out," Devil Jose warned. "Ifen thet's whut they's up to they's in fer one helluva fight."

He turned to his three nephews and told them to take their guns and take up positions in the barn. This would give them an opportunity to catch some of the Deatons in a crossfire. He handed a pistol each to James and Charles. He told the boys that he was indeed sorry they were caught in the middle but that they had no place to go and nothing to do but defend themselves as best they could.

Just as the last bolt was being closed on the cabin doors, several shots rang out in the night.

"They can't do no damage to them logs, and we'uns air safe in hyar," Joe assured them. "The onliest thing thet worries me is ifen they set fire to the cabin. One of ye boys git to each winder. Make damn shore them guns air loaded. Don't shoot until ye're shore of killin' a Deaton!"

Once again, Devil Joe turned to the two visitors from Lexington. He told them that this was not their fight and that he would understand if they wanted to try getting out through the gap in their Jeep. Neither of the two options open to them seemed to offer much hope, but the two young men elected to stick it out with Callahan and his family.

"We'uns all is likely gonna git kilt," the mountain man cautioned. "Them Deatons been a-plannin' this fer a long time. I knowed hit was jist too quiet tonight. Dammit to hell! I shoulda had one of the boys a-guardin' the mouth of the holler and another up on the ridge, but hit's too late now."

Joe kept an eye on every position in the cabin as he walked from window to window. After the initial volley of bullets hit the house, the gunfire from outside had dwindled to just an occasional shot. Callahan judged that the Deatons were firing just enough to keep them pinned down while they readied some sort of surprise attack. After an hour of waiting with just an occasional shot fired at the cabin, someone heard a wagon coming along the creek. Opening a special peephole cut in between two logs, Devil Joe took a look outside to see if he could make out what was happening.

"I knowed hit," he half-muttered to himself. "They's got a wagon loaded with rocks and hay. They's a-draggin' hit up the hill. When they turn thet thing loose, hit'll go plumb through this cabin."

Turning to his wife, he said, "Betty, ye take the girls and the younguns into thet back room. I know them Deatons! They's aimin' to set fire to thet wagonload of hay and bust hit into the cabin wall. We'll burn like rats ifen we stay in hyar, and ifen we try to git out they aim to shoot us down."

In a matter of moments everyone in the cabin knew what was happening. From a distance up the hill came the shouted instructions, "Let 'er go!" followed by the rumbling sound of the wagon as it bore down on the cabin. The impact of the burning wagon crashing into the side of the cabin gouged out a large hole. Immediately, a hail of bullets poured through the opening.

Inside the cabin there was utter confusion. Three of Devil Joe's sons died in the first volley of shots. Charles Davis was hit in the head and chest, dying instantly. The two daughters-in-law died with their children in their arms. Joe's wife, Betty, tried to run from the burning cabin carrying a third grandchild but was cut down by a bullet before she could get off the porch. James fired into the darkness until the pistol Devil Joe had given him was empty.

As the Deatons continued pouring shots into the burning cabin, Devil Joe's voice could be heard above the noise, "Dammit to hell, they's a-killin' muh whole family! How many's alive in hyar?"

"Only five of us air left, Pa," came Jamie's voice in reply. "We'uns air agonna burn like rats!"

"Like hell we air!" shouted Devil Joe. He then turned to James Taylor and told him to take the body of his friend, Charles, get it in the Jeep and head up the road for the gap and Hypen. Next, he addressed his three remaining sons.

"Hyar's what we'uns air a-gonna do," he directed. "Take two pistols apiece and after this boy gits his friend's body outten the side door, we'uns charge them Deatons through the front yard."

As James dragged Charles Davis' body through the side door of the burning cabin, Devil Joe Callahan and his three sons lunged into the front yard with their guns blazing. Two made it to the gate before being killed. The third managed to kill two Deatons before he fell in the hail of bullets. James took a last look at Devil Joe as he put Charles' body into the Jeep and started the motor.

Devil Joe was virtually a madman. Silhouetted against the light of the burning cabin, he shouted the rebel yell and danced wildly in the middle of the yard as he fired into the darkness around him. James knew that the Deaton bullets must be hitting Joe, but he appeared to ignore them. As James looked back, the hulk of a man stopped and appeared to sway as he looked toward the burning cabin and the bodies of his wife and grandson lying on the porch. The last James saw was Devil Joe falling...falling in the light of a bright moon and the burning cabin...next to the bodies of two of his sons. As he fell to the ground, his voice rang loud and clear, "Damn ever Deaton whut ever lived!"

The Jeep had just cleared the yard when James saw flashes of gunfire from the barn. One of Joe's nephews was still alive and shooting at the Deatons. As the Jeep bounced into the ruts of the wagon road, the Deatons directed their fire toward it. However, not being accustomed to shooting at such a fast moving target, only two bullets struck the vehicle.

James drove as he had never driven before. Sometimes he was in the wagon road, sometimes he was out. The body of his friend, Charles, was wedged into the front seat beside him. As he neared the gap, the fog began to settle on the mountain, and James prayed, "Lord please let this be the right road to get us out of this place."

Soon, he passed through the gap into the damp air of the fog. Ahead through the fog was a sight he had thought he might never see again. Two sets of automobile headlights! Careening around a curve and onto a blacktop road, he realized that somewhere in the gap or in the fog, he had found the road he sought...the road that led him back to reality.

Suddenly, he became aware of sirens and the flashing lights of two police cars. He stopped the Jeep, and two police officers approached him. He recognized the state trooper and the deputy sheriff he had seen when he and Charles had first pulled into Hypen.

"Son, what's going on?" State Trooper John Combs asked. "You were driving like a wild man, and what has happened to your friend?"

"The Deatons killed Charles," James blurted out. "Devil Joe Callahan's cabin is burning down on the creek, and the Deatons are killing his whole family. Let's go back to help them...to see if any of them might still be alive."

The state trooper and the deputy tried to calm the young man, who was babbling on about the incident and waving the old pistol he had brought out with him.

"Give me that old gun," Trooper Combs said. "Where did you get it, anyway?"

"Devil Joe gave it to me," James replied. "I must have put it in my belt when I left the cabin. Let's go back and see if we can help the Callahans."

"Now, let's just calm down, son," Deputy Sheriff Clark joined in. "You'll have to come back with us to the sheriff's office so we can go over all this. After all, we have a dead man here that we need to get into town."

"But that's an awful mess down at the Callahans' cabin," James insisted. "Why can't we go back...or at least get some-body to go back and see if we can help Devil Joe?"

"The best reason I can think of is that Devil Joe Callahan and his family have all been dead for more than 80 years," the deputy said. "Now, just try to calm down and come with us."

Trooper Combs left his patrol car and drove the Jeep back to Hypen, taking the body of Charles Davis to the coroner's office. Deputy Clark took James Taylor in his vehicle and drove him back to the sheriff's office. Once inside, the deputy gave his account of the event to Sheriff Walter Back.

"John Combs and I were parked over at the gap when this

boy came roaring out of Devil's Holler on that gravel road not an hour after he left the filling station. Sheriff, it's a miracle he didn't wreck that Jeep the way he was driving. When we finally got him stopped, he was crying and cursing, 'I'll kill ever' damn Deaton I find.' He acted like he was crazy, waving that old pistol around. I believe he would have shot us, but the gun was empty. As you can see, he has blood all over him, and his clothes and hair are burned. Whatever it was, he's been through something awful. He kept saying, 'They're all dead, Devil Joe and his whole family. They're all dead! The Deatons set fire to the cabin and killed every one of them!' His buddy was in the Jeep with him, but he's dead. Combs took the Davis boy's body to the coroner's office; he'll bring you a report later. There're at least 10 witnesses, including Combs and me, who saw and talked to those two boys, and we all saw them leave Golf's filling station not over an hour before he came back out of Devil's Holler.

"There's something bad wrong here," he continued. "You know it's less than three miles over to the old Callahan place. And you know, Sheriff, it was exactly 82 years ago today that Devil Joe Callahan and his family were killed and burned by the Deatons in Devil's Holler."

"Sheriff, it's the God's truth," James tried to explain. "I don't know how we got back there in 1879, but we did. I didn't know anything about the Callahan-Deaton feud until we went through the fog and down the creek to Devil Joe's store and cabin. He told us about the feud. We were there a few days before the Deatons raided Joe's cabin. When they set fire to the cabin, most of Devil Joe's family was killed and Charles was shot twice. I dragged his body out of the burning cabin, put it in the Jeep and drove up the creek, praying that I could find the right road. The Deatons shot at the Jeep, but I didn't stop. When I got to the gap, I ran into the fog again. I guess God must have guided me because, somehow, I got back on the road that leads into town. That's when your deputy and the state policeman stopped the Jeep and brought me here."

"Son, you don't really expect me to believe that story, do

you?" the Sheriff asked. "We don't have fog around here this time of the year. Besides, you boys were gone from that filling station for no more than an hour. You couldn't have seen Devil Joe Callahan and his family because they've all been dead over 80 years. The feuds have been over around here for at least 70 years. And what in the hell has fog got to do with this anyway?"

"All I know is that when we went through that patch of fog at the gap over there on Route 28, everything changed," James insisted. "The timber had never been cut, the stream was larger than the topographic map shows, the air seemed different and the road was only dirt with nothing but wagon tracks, not gravel.

"I don't understand it either, but Sheriff, I tell you Charles and I spent 10 days at Devil Joe's place. We went there on Friday, July 12th. I haven't seen a calendar, but this has to be July 22, 1961."

"Son, you're crazy!" the sheriff insisted. "Look at this calendar on my desk. Today is July 12, 1961, not July 22! I don—"

"Sheriff," James interrupted, "there's one other thing, and I don't understand it either. During the fighting, after the cabin had been set on fire, Devil Joe said to me, "Son, I didn't tell ye this afore, 'cause I knowed ye wouldn't believe me. I'm agonna die in this fight is why I'm a-tellin' ye now. I have the power of prophecy, thet's how I knowed ye two boys wuz a-tellin' the truth. I don't know how ye got back hyar to 1879, but yer friend is dead. Ye'll get away yerself, but yer agonna spend the rest of yer life in misery. 'Cause they ain't nobody agonna believe yer story when ye leave hyar. Ye'll live zactly 10 yars from now. I ain't a prayin' man, but may God help ye!'"

"I know that Devil Joe Callahan and most of his family were killed and his cabin burned by the Deatons in 1879," said the sheriff. "Fifteen of the Callahans, what was left of them, are buried above the cabin site. And I have to admit that Callahan tradition says Devil Joe could see the future. But, son, nothing you've told us proves what you say is true.

I sure can't figure out where you got that old pistol, and I sure don't understand why you killed your friend. But you're going to have to stand trial for murder if this is all the evidence you have."

"Sheriff, maybe I do have some more evidence that will convince you," James recalled. "I can prove that we were at Devil Joe's cabin in 1879. I had a camera with me and took several pictures of Devil Joe and his family while we were there. The camera and film are in the Jeep. Get the film developed, and you will see I'm telling the truth."

"All right, all right," the sheriff answered. "We'll have the film developed. I sure hope you're right because this is getting crazier every minute."

The sheriff told a deputy to take the film to Bishop's Drug Store and to tell them that he wanted the pictures in an hour.

A short time later State Policeman John Combs came to the sheriff's office with the coroner's report. The bullet removed from the chest of Charles Taylor was a .36 caliber fired from a muzzle-loading Colt. Combs also said that there were two bullet holes in the Jeep and were very likely made by a .69 caliber weapon.

"Sheriff," Combs continued, "here's something else that's hard to believe. Look at the initials carved in the grip of this old pistol Taylor was carrying: DJC, Devil Joe Callahan. And look on this side, 11 notches! Callahan tradition says that Devil Joe killed 11 men."

The sheriff admitted that there were a lot of circumstances pointing to the truth of what Taylor said. The major problem was that they had a dead man on their hands and needed something more concrete if they were to solve the mystery to the satisfaction of all concerned. The parents of Taylor and those of Davis were notified in Lexington. The sheriff asked them to keep the information out of the news until they could get more substantial facts to go on. He also called in John Callahan, a local feed merchant and family authority on the Callahan clan's history. He felt that Callahan could help validate or invalidate the pictures being developed from Taylor's film by comparing them with some of the old photographs in the merchant's possession.

In a very short time John Callahan arrived, bringing with him the old Callahan family pictures the sheriff had requested. Arriving very nearly at the same time was the deputy who had been dispatched to have Taylor's film developed. The sheriff went over Taylor's story once again, for the benefit of John Callahan. He explained that the young man claimed to have made some photographs of Devil Joe Callahan and members of his family only an hour or two ago. John made it clear that he didn't believe the story for a moment, knowing for certain that Devil Joe and all his immediate family perished many years ago. However, he agreed to have a look at the pictures and make a comparison between them and the old tintypes of Devil Joe and his family which he had brought with him. As he laid the old and the new pictures side by side, a startled look came over his face.

"My God, Sheriff!" Callahan exclaimed. "I see it, but I still can't believe it! That's Devil Joe, all right. He's wearing those two big pistols they say he always carried. And there's a picture of my great-aunt Melinda. Here's one showing Luke, Billy and Jamie standing by the spring. Sheriff, we've both drunk water from that spring many times. And here's a picture of Joe and his wife, Betty. This one shows the cabin and the hillside behind it. That hillside looks just the same today, except the cabin is gone and so are those big trees that surrounded it."

Turning to look at James Taylor, Callahan asked, "Son, how in the name of God did you get these pictures? These are the real Callahans, but you couldn't have made them just today. They've all been dead 40 years and most of them even longer, and you couldn't be a day over 20! My great-aunt Melinda was the last of these in the pictures to die, and she passed away in 1920. My Lord, I just don't believe it!"

The sheriff advised John Callahan that it would be best not to say anything about the pictures or Taylor's story to anyone outside. The descendant of Devil Joe didn't need any prompting to be aware of that fact. He knew that no one would believe a word of such a wild tale in the first place.

James Taylor admitted that were it not for the burns he had suffered, the old pistol he had brought back and the pictures he had made while there, he would think his mind was playing tricks on him. Ironically, because he knew his experience had been real, it was even more difficult for his mind to hold onto reality. The comparison of the pictures concluded the questioning of Taylor for the time being. Taylor was placed in a cell for the night after a doctor had treated his burns and given him a sedative.

The sheriff's office had notified the families of both Taylor and Davis. Arrangements were made to send the body of Charles Davis home to Lexington.

The coroner's report concluded that Davis had died instantly from the bullet wounds. It went on to say that one bullet struck him in the head while the other entered the chest. The report also noted that the wounds were made by .36 caliber bullets.

First and second degree burns on the body indicated that it had been in or very near intense heat, but that the burns occurred after death. Broken and abraded skin indicated that the body had been dragged along the ground for a short distance. The report was signed by Silas Johnson, Coroner of Albany County, Kentucky.

Indicted for the murder of his friend, Charles Davis, Taylor was ordered held over for trial at the next term of circuit court. Taylor's parents retained two Lexington attorneys to defend their son.

At the trial, the only tangible evidence presented was the old revolver and the photographs made from the film Taylor had with him when he was first apprehended by the police. The prosecuting attorney maintained that Taylor could have found the old revolver somewhere in Devil's Hollow. The photographs which the young man claimed to have taken of Devil Joe and his family were also dismissed as evidence. The prosecutors contended that with all the modern technology at our disposal the photographs could have been faked. State Trooper Combs and Deputy Sheriff Clark were never allowed to testify. Authorities contended that all the information possessed by the two officers was basically hearsay and circumstantial at best.

The jury did not reach a verdict that dealt with the question that most folks wanted answered. They could not bring themselves to believe the truth of Taylor's story, that he and Charles Davis really did return to 1879 and take part in the Callahan-Deaton feud. Had they so concluded, they would have had no choice but to free Taylor of the charge. Neither could they bring themselves to believe that James Taylor willfully murdered his best friend. They were left with one alternative: to find him not guilty by reason of insanity. They recommended that he undergo psychiatric examination and be turned over to a mental hospital.

Taylor was moved to a mental hospital where he was pronounced criminally insane. He remained in that hospital until his death on July 12, 1971, exactly 10 years from the date he claimed to have been involved in the fight at Devil Joe Callahan's cabin, the exact number of years allocated to him by Devil Joe's prediction.

Many people who witnessed the trial of James Taylor were convinced that the jury failed to do its duty. These people maintained that the decision reached served the same purpose as a guilty verdict. These observers said that the members of the jury were really afraid to make a decision in the case and were even more afraid to face up to what might have been the real facts.

The strange events of 1961 have been investigated many times by competent people, and none have been able to give a plausible explanation. During the final years that Taylor lived, he was questioned many times. His story never changed.

Descendants of the Callahan family still live in Albany County. All of them know the legend, but most are reluctant to talk about the feud and the mass killing of Devil Joe and his family that tragic night in 1879.

County records contain several facts that are associated with the various feuds which occurred in Albany County between 1870 and 1890. Diligent research shows that the

Callahans and the Deatons battled back and forth for more than 10 years, and it is estimated that at least 35 people from the two clans were killed during this time. Perhaps the most interesting item turned up in our search was a faded letter still owned by a great-grandson of Devil Joe Callahan. The letter was dated July 26, 1879, and was postmarked Hypen, Kentucky. This would have been 14 days after the fight that claimed so many Callahan lives. Devil Joe's nephew had written the letter to one of Devil Joe's daughters living in Ohio. He told her of the tragic fight, but what makes the letter even more intriguing is his mention of the strangers who had come to visit Devil Joe. He noted that the two strangers not only talked funny and dressed peculiar, but that they arrived in a horseless wagon. He even enclosed a drawing of the "wagon." It is a good representation of a Jeep, rendered sixty years before that vehicle was ever manufactured. He told his kinswoman that one of the strangers had also been killed in the fight and that the other had dragged him out, put him in the horseless wagon and drove away toward the gap with the Deatons shooting at him. The Callahan writing the letter had been one of the three nephews Devil Joe had sent to the barn before the fight started. The other two had been killed.

In October 1961, about two months after Taylor's trial, three men from Hypen were using a metal detector as they searched for artifacts around the old Callahan cabin site. Buried about six inches beneath the surface of the ground, they found a rusty old pocket knife. After they cleaned up the old knife they could read the engraved initials J.S.T. (James Stephen Taylor?). In front of the cabin site near the old wagon roadbed, they found another interesting artifact buried about five inches below the surface. It was a 1959 high school class ring. Engraved inside the band was the name Charles E. Davis. Geologists say that a ring or a pocket knife dropped in this area would take 75 to 100 years to be buried that far beneath the surface, based on the known weather conditions and slow buildup of topsoil. The three men who found these items still live in Hypen. They are reputable folks, and all indications are that they have told the truth about their find. The ring and the knife were returned to the parents of the boys.

The Taylor and Davis families confirmed that neither of the two had ever been in Albany County before the incident. Taylor's attorneys used the information about the knife and the ring in their efforts to get a new trial for their client, but the courts ruled that these did not offer sufficient new evidence, that the items could have been lost at the site in 1961. No mention was made as to how they rationalized the depth to which both items had become buried in just a matter of days.

The 1871 model Colt revolver with Devil Joe Callahan's initials and the 11 notches carved on the grip remained at the county sheriff's office in Hypen until recently, when it mysteriously disappeared.

John Callahan still has the color photographs of Devil Joe and his family which Taylor claimed to have taken when he went back in time.

Parts of the old wagon road that crossed the gap into Devil's Hollow can still be seen. All of these are nagging remnants of what would seem to be proof that James Taylor told the truth...that he and Charles Davis really did go back in time to 1879 and really did take part in the Callahan-Deaton feud.

EPILOGUE

The crack of gunfire, the cursing voices are stilled. The feud is legend now. The fear, the hatred, the strange code that dictated revenge at any cost...all lie dormant among the peaceful woods and streams that still endure the Devil's Hollow. In the valley once filled with pain and suffering there is tranquility, and silence reigns.

Looking at the old fruit trees, rose bushes and the remaining stone foundations that once supported buildings, it is hard to realize that violence, fear and death once surrounded a cabin that stood here in 1879. It is a quiet and lonely place now.

If the earth could talk, what would it tell of the 15 who now rest in silence on the hill above the place where the cabin stood? Could it speak to us of the anguish and pain suffered by James Taylor, caught in a time and a circumstance he could not control? And what of Charles Davis? Perhaps his was the strangest puzzle of all. A young man who died in a time before he was born, not understanding why or even how he came to be there. Perhaps Devil Joe Callahan's comment was a masterpiece of understatement when he said, "They's some strange things whut happens to people."

The old Callahan cabin stood in the back center of this photograph.

Golden Wings

Little Jennie Freemon was born with a congenital heart defect. It restricted her physical activity to a few hours each day. On what was to be her final day, Jennie's mother was visiting a neighbor. The little girl took advantage of this absence of mother's restraint to play harder than she should have. Jennie exerted herself, and her little heart was unable to stand the strain.

When Mrs. Freemon returned home, she found little Jennie in a coma. She rushed her to a hospital, where Jennie was immediately placed in the intensive care unit. The cardiologist sent the distraught parents home and began extensive examinations to determine the damage to the little girl's heart. Within a few hours, he realized the short life could not be saved. He notified the parents and waited for them in Jennie's room.

As the young couple came down the corridor for what would be a final visit with their little girl, the hospital was unusually quiet...a quiet and stillness like the air before a storm. Small snowflakes hit the windows and melted away, gone forever, like the short life in Room 712 would be soon. When the parents entered the room, the doctor shook his head sadly and walked out.

Responding to her mother's touch, frail Jennie opened her eyes and said, "Mommy, I went to heaven and saw Jesus. He told me to come back and tell you and Daddy goodbye and for you not to worry."

Mrs. Freemon hugged her child and agreed, thinking that she was delirious. Minutes later, Jennie raised up in bed with the most beautiful look of rapture on her face that her parents had ever seen. Looking at her mother, Jennie said,

"Jesus has come back for me, Mommy. See him just above you?" Reaching her arms upward, the little girl seemed to relax; then, with her skin turning pale, she fell back on the bed and was still.

The father rushed from the room and returned with the doctor, who checked Jennie's pulse and eyelids and started to pull the sheet up over the child's face. He noticed that one of her hands was clinched tightly. Gently pulling the fingers apart, he was amazed to find that Jennie was holding a small pair of beautiful golden wings.

The wings were later evaluated by several jewelry experts who agreed that they were made of gold; but the intricate art work was an unknown design.

The Eye — Cherokee's Spirit Place

The Eye

At the southern tip of the Pine Mountain Range near Frakes, Kentucky, there is an unusual and rarely frequented ridge which the Cherokee Indians avoid. They call it Wa-he-ta-na...the spirit place. Since the first white pioneers visited it, recorded history tells us that this area has never changed.

While visiting this remote, rock-strewn ridge covered with small timber, vegetation and brambles, I felt deep silence. There were unusual faded colors and smells which held faint traces of indefinable perfumes. It is an eerie, mysterious place. A forgotten fairyland exists here, lost in the depths of time.

Chiseled into the solid rock are numerous deep carvings

and raised objects that erosion does not seem to affect. A stone chair waits at the end of a natural amphitheater, seemingly for the return of a long forgotten teacher. A bear's head, a reclining lion, horse's tracks, the outline of a deer, a hand, a human skull, squares and circles disappear only to reappear. Half moons, one within another, are joined to a triangle. And there are several other odd, out-of-place stone formations which are parts of this fantastic, haunting, beautiful and dreamlike spot. It is like a scene from another world or another time...a wonder that defies explanation.

Above it all, possibly on perpetual guard, looms a large opening through the cliff side. Known as "The Eye," it is inscrutable, forbidding, silent, defensively watching. It seems to follow one regardless of the direction from which it is viewed, jealously guarding its ancient secrets. This awesome phenomenon is strangely out of place with nature in this jumbled labyrinth of stone. No similar formations exist for miles in any direction. When you touch the sandstone overhangs, you disturb the dust of centuries, since erosion has not affected this curiosity in over 200 years of recorded history.

The Eye is native stone...not a man-made object, yet it does not appear to be natural. The Eye is in a stone formation that slants at a 45-degree angle, although no other cliffs in the area do this. It defies all laws of man-made or natural construction. With a little imagination, one can visualize an ancient giant pushing his finger through the cliff to form this gigantic hole.

Even the forests below the ridge and The Eye seem unusually dark and quiet. There are nearby streams so deep within the cliffs that the sun does not reach them until late morning and is gone again by early afternoon.

Local people tell me that the atmosphere seems to change after sunset and that strange, unidentifiable sounds can sometimes be heard at night along the ridge. After visiting this place, it is understandable why the Indians avoided it and never stopped, preferring to camp and hunt miles away. Even today, few hunters or hikers visit after dark, and no wildlife is ever seen along this ridge. It is a quiet and lonely place.

As I walked alone along an ancient path on this high, jut-ted mass of earth and stone, I seemed to hear—as if from a great distance, possibly from another time—faint sounds, the whisperings of invisible crowds. It is like the rustling of past lives, flowing, ebbing, disappearing, returning, evaporating at the slightest sound made by any intruder, whether man, a breeze or even a ray of sunshine. The fleeting shadows cast by sunlight among the rocks are like retreating souls growing lonely.

I felt out of place, an unwelcome intruder, being silently observed, not belonging and not wanted. There are secrets there which belong to the past, to others, not to be disturbed.

Ancient Hebrew Coins Unearthed

Picture A
Interpretation of Picture A—
"Year 2 of the Freedom of Israel"

Picture B
Shows a building representing
the Jewish Temple in Jerusalem.

According to most theories, Columbus discovered America in 1492. But evidence keeps accumulating to prove that Columbus was actually a latecomer to North America. One example of this evidence is the discovery of ancient Hebrew coins in Kentucky and other areas in the midwest.

One Sunday morning in 1952, Robert Fox, of Park City, was on his way to church. As he walked across a freshly plowed field near his home, the sun reflected against something shiny sticking from a clod of dirt. Cox picked up the object and started to throw it away when, at first glance, the metal appeared to be only an old button. Strangely, however, he didn't. After church he took it home, washed it off and discovered it was a coin covered with odd inscriptions.

Fox, an avid Bible reader, recalled some pictures of old

Hebrew coins in a Biblical dictionary he owned. From those pictures he recognized a coin that looked like the one he found. It had been struck over 1,840 years ago in either the first or second Jewish revolt against the Romans.

On one side of the coin, made of copper and a little smaller than an American half-dollar, was a building representing the temple of Jerusalem which the Romans had destroyed. There was a six-pointed star over the center. Letters at the left of the temple were an abbreviation for the name Shemeon (Simon), the real name of the Jewish leader in the last revolt in A.D. 133. Opposite was a semicircle of letters with what appeared to be a shock of wheat in the center. These characters read: "Year 2 of the Freedom of Israel."

The age of the coin was positively established by Dr. Ralph Marcus of the University of Chicago, a man recognized as the leading scholar on Hellenistic culture. He determined that the coin was struck by Simon Bar Kokba, the leader of the second revolt against the Romans. The year was A.D. 133.

Other Hebrew and Roman coins have been found in Kentucky, Tennessee and Illinois. Judge John Haywood, in his book *Natural and Aboriginal History of Tennessee*, written in 1823, tells of Roman coins being plowed up by farmers near Jackson, Tennessee. About 1940, Joseph Cray, of Pleasure Ridge Park, Kentucky, found a Hebrew coin of the same vintage (A.D. 133) while plowing a garden. Other coins of the same type were found near Hopkinsville in 1950, and also near Chicago, Illinois.

Dr. Barry Fell, Epigraphic Society, Arlington, Massachusetts, an expert on ancient coins and artifacts; Dr. Cyrus Gordan, Chairman of the Department of Mediterranean Studies, Brandeis University, Waltham, Massachusetts; and Israel T. Naamani, a professor at the University of Louisville, Louisville, Kentucky, another expert on Hebrew coinage, have all authenticated the coin Robert Fox found. Its value is estimated to be between $500 and $1,000.

Dr. Fell and Dr. Gordan believe that a Jewish colony may have existed over 2,000 years ago in Kentucky with a possible trade route from the Gulf of Mexico to the Great Lakes.

This theory has never been proven, so the 1,800-year-old coins' appearances throughout the midwestern United States remain a mystery.

Jewish history says this about Bar Kokba, the hero who minted the coins: Bar Kokba, literally meaning "Son of the Star," was the chief of insurgents who led a revolt to regain Jewish independence or, at least, their right to practice their religion freely. To pay his soldiers, Bar Kokba struck his own coins. During the revolt, he exercised almost kingly powers and, indeed, announced that he was the Messiah.

The revolt, starting in A.D. 132 and lasting only until 135, was short but bloody. Finally, it was crushed by the Romans, and all Hebrew synagogues were destroyed.

Startling Contents of Indian Mounds

During the Great Depression of the 1930s, most people would work at anything in order to earn a living. There was a strip of land along the Ohio River which had several Indian burial mounds on it that had never been investigated. At the time of this incident in 1932, there were no laws or regulations against digging into known Indian burial sites. These particular burial mounds had a known existence of over 150 years in recorded history.

Four men decided to dig into these mounds in search of Indian artifacts which they could sell to museums for a small price.

James Pence and Orville Taylor were sharecroppers in the neighborhood, while the other two men, Charles Wilson and William Mueller, were from Louisville, Kentucky, about 50 miles away.

Realizing that the excavation would take several weeks, Mueller and Wilson set up a campsite near the mounds. At first, nothing unusual happened. After the digging had been going on for several days, Mueller began to complain of hearing noises at night. The other men kept saying that it was just his imagination, but Mueller insisted he could hear men speaking in a strange language. Days went by and the mound gradually disappeared. Mueller became more and more depressed, but desperately needing the money the relics would bring, he continued digging.

Late one afternoon, the men made the initial break into what appeared to be a man-made burial cavern. Since it was late in the day, they decided to wait until the next morning to open the chamber.

During the night Mueller claimed that he could still hear the voices. Not only could he hear, but he could also see the ghosts of Indians and strangely dressed white men who carried metal shields, swords, spears and helmets. He kept telling Wilson it was dangerous to continue digging. Wilson also was beginning to have second thoughts about breaking into the burial cavern. Both men spent a sleepless night, and, although Wilson never saw any apparitions, he said later that he did hear the voices.

Early the next morning, the four men went to work breaking down the supporting wall of the chamber. When the wall fell away, they saw the bodies of several Indians sitting on rock benches in a circle along the inside walls. The bodies, dressed in full battle gear, were perfectly preserved and looked like they had been in the chamber only a few days. Mueller, already on the verge of emotional collapse, finally passed into mental oblivion when he saw the body of the huge man sitting in the center of the circle. This warrior was armed with a large metal shield, spear, knife, sword and helmet, and wore a knee-length skirt made of leather. But the feature that was most unusual was the warrior's long blond hair and beard. With Mueller in the lead, the four men backed away from the figures. Then they began to run down the long, sandy strip of land until they finally fell from sheer exhaustion. Mueller's mind was completely gone, and he kept repeating, "Their leader was a Viking warrior."

The other three men decided to wait to investigate the chamber further until after they could get Mueller to a doctor. Regaining their composure after several hours, they returned to the excavation site. Nothing had been disturbed. Taking their time, they began to examine the bodies, questioning their own sanity on what they had found. Wilson started to examine the body of the Indian medicine man. Suddenly he began to scream. He had removed a perfectly preserved leather pouch from the body's waist and, upon opening it, saw dozens of Indian-head pennies...he realized that what he was looking at was impossible. He ran outside, grabbed a pistol from his pack, put the barrel into his mouth and shot himself.

By now, Pence and Taylor were so panic-stricken that they left the cavern and ran home. When they were finally able to stop shaking, they notified the authorities. The site was roped off, and the sheriff's office started an investigation.

When the investigators entered the cavern, there were no bodies. All that remained, placed in a neat pile near the outer wall, was a leather pouch half filled with Indian-head pennies, a metal shield (later identified at a large university as Viking), and a beautiful, silver peace pipe.

Because of the unusual aspects of the mound, the sheriff had the highway department level the area with bulldozers. Pence and Taylor moved away and were never seen in the area again.

The metal shield was given to a museum in Washington, D.C. The silver peace pipe eventually disappeared from the sheriff's office, and the whereabouts of the Indian-head pennies is unknown.

There are numerous questions which remain unanswered concerning this incident. Had the Indians and the Viking warrior smoked the pipe of peace? Where did the silver peace pipe come from...Indians did not know metallurgy. Was there more than one Viking? There's no logical way to explain Indian-head pennies in an Indian grave that was over two hundred years old, yet several members of the sheriff's office, among others, saw the coins Wilson found in the medicine man's pouch. What caused Mueller's premonition of danger? Where did the bodies from the burial chamber go after Wilson killed himself and the other two men ran?

Those who scoff at this story may find credence in additional evidence found at a later date.

In 1940, Elias Calloway was hunting squirrels when he found a spring on the hill directly above the burial chamber location. Although hundreds of men had hunted this area for years, no one had ever seen this spring, which had, evidently, just suddenly appeared. While Calloway investigated this source of fresh water, he noticed three flat rocks—about two feet square. They appeared to have writing on them and seemed out of place on the hillside. After scraping away the moss and debris, he carried the rocks home. A thorough cleaning revealed some curious symbols and markings which he was unable to decipher. He contacted a museum, which sent two archaeologists to the Calloway home.

The men were totally unprepared for what they found. The rocks were Viking runic stones which told the story of a ship's crew that had been wrecked on the coast of what is now Virginia. The crew had traveled west until they came to a large river (apparently the Ohio). During their wanderings, several had died of diseases; others had been killed by Indians. The remaining few made friends with a group of Indians along the river. The Viking warrior found in the burial chamber had apparently been the last to die.

Do these stones explain Indian legends told to the first white settlers who came to the Falls of the Ohio (now Louisville) in 1778? These legends spoke of white with corn-colored hair, who, years before, had built a fort on the high ridge near the mouth of what is now 14 Mile Creek. The legend went on to say that all these while men had been killed or died through natural causes.

Nine Mysterious Graves

In western Kentucky, there is a burial site of nine graves bearing several unusual features. There are no written records available, so the history of this particular burial site had to be traced back through people who live in the area to its discovery in 1890. This discovery took place when timber was being cut in the area, and the leaves and other debris covering the graves was disturbed.

The nine graves are laid out in a straight line, all pointing east. They are all the same length, approximately seven feet, and each is surrounded by a circle of stones. Each stone is a uniform shape and about the size of a one-quart containers. They appear to have been smoothed to a circular shape by the action of water rather than being carved or chipped, although the closest river is the Cumberland, more than two miles away. Each grave has about the same number of stones circling it.

The most remarkable feature of the burial site is that the graves look as if they were recently filled. There is no erosion, and they have not sunk to form cavities as most graves do after a few years.

Indian mounds around this site have been opened for investigation; but strangely enough, this line of graves has not been disturbed. The commonly accepted theory is that the graves are those of a race of people who pre-date American Indians, possibly Hebrew or Welsh.

What these graves contain, what race the people were or when the burial took place remain a mystery. They had not been disturbed as late as 1979, and I have yet to see another burial site which is in any manner similar.

The Amazing Kewanee Stone

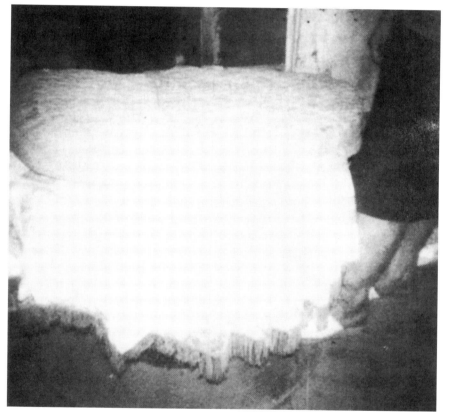

I first met the Jess Coleman family of Kewanee, Pike County, Kentucky, in June 1978. It was after I had read a newspaper clipping about the strange carved rock they found following a flood in March and April of 1977. The artifact would probably not have been discovered without the extensive soil erosion that took place during the flood. During the visit, they let me view and photograph the unusual stone.

The relic, measuring about 36 inches long, 22 inches wide, 8 inches thick, and weighing approximately 200 pounds, is carved in the shape of a coiled serpent with its head in the center. The circles or coils found only on top of the stone are not uniform in size, varying from about 3½ inches to 6 inches. They are connected by what appear to be inverted letters. The stone looks like limestone with several "veins," or heavy traces of iron, running through it. The edges around the entire carving are smooth as if it had been polished. Its age and origin are unknown.

We hiked to the exact site where the Colemans discovered the stone. It was not the original position of the stone, since it had moved down the hill a distance of several feet because of erosion. The location is unusual, being about halfway up a hill which has an elevation of 1,000 feet. The area is about 25 yards long, 25 feet wide and almost completely level. The stone was lying at the lower edge of this area when found. Several rock specimens along the hillside were checked, and only red and grey sandstone were found. It is almost certain that the carved stone did not come from this area of the mountain.

Photos of the relic have been sent to The Epigraphic Society, Arlington, Massachusetts; the Department of Anthropology at the University of Kentucky, Lexington; and the Archaeology Survey, University of Louisville. So far, no one has been able to make a positive identification of the stone although several theories have been advanced.

It has been suggested that the stone indicated the location of buried treasure or was a boundary marker or gravestone of early pioneers. It could even be an Indian religious totem, an Aztec Sun God symbol, an Indian calendar stone, a symbol left by the Spanish explorers in 1632, or a trail sign left by the French when they claimed the Northwest Territory. It has even been suggested that it was left as a marker by the legendary John Swift when he supposedly mined silver in this area in the 1760s. Other opinions about the stone's origin have been given, but its true meaning will remain unknown until someone can make a positive identification or decipher it.

Mountain of the "Spirit Water"

In southern Kentucky, there is a one acre square on the top of a mountain that maintains a constant 80-degree temperature. No snow remains on the ground regardless of the amount of snowfall, and, although rain falls in the area, it quickly evaporates. As far as we can determine, this phenomenon occurs nowhere else in the world.

Four large round depressions, exactly 10 yards apart, can be seen here; and they form a perfect square. These indentations appear to have been made by a large object of tremendous weight. According to Indian legend, they were made by a huge shining bird over 2,000 years ago. People have tried to fill the depressions with soil, leaves and stones dozens of times, but they are always empty the next day. No one knows where the debris goes.

Surrounding rock formations show signs of intense heat, yet geologists state that no volcanoes have ever existed in the area. Chemists, geologists, engineers and agriculturists have tried, without success, every known scientific method to determine what caused this strange phenomenon.

Soil and rock samples have been obtained from a depth of 20 feet. The tests for mineral content show that all samples were free of any of the 92 known elements. Different trees, shrubs and grasses have been planted, only to grow for a short time, then die.

When the first pioneers entered the area in the 1770s, they were told about this strange mountaintop by local Indians. Legend says that a big, shinning bird landed there every few years. Gods who wore bright clothes and carried strange tools would come out of the bird's mouth, walk around, then go back into its mouth; and the bird would fly away. The last sighting had been several years prior to the white man's entry into the area.

Once in their legends, the Indians spoke of a man who approached the great bird when it landed. This man, a chief named Huraken who was renowned for his bravery, walked to within a few feet of the great bird while the tribe watched from the valley below. Suddenly, a long coiled arm grabbed him, and the bird flew away. Huraken was never seen or heard of again.

Legend also tells of a spring of water that appeared among the rocks after the first sighting. The water from the spring seemed to affect wild animals that drank it. They grew larger, appeared healthier and lived longer than normal. The Indians called this "Spirit Water" and, being superstitious, would not drink it.

The earliest mention by a white man of this place with its unusual spring and depressions is found in a diary kept by Silas Collins from 1779 to 1785. He tells of gathering dried wood at mid-winter on top of this mountain. He also grazed his cattle in this area during winter because the trees, grass and shrubbery stayed green although snow drifts were piled five feet high around it. Collins noted that his livestock lived longer and were healthier after they drank water from the spring. This water, like the soil, shows no known minerals. That, too, science is at a loss to explain.

The area is deserted now and seldom visited, but the four depressions and the spring are the same as they were when the Indians first saw the huge bird make them. Modern science doesn't seem to be any closer to the answers today than were the Indians 2,000 years ago.

Was this mountaintop visited by aliens with scientific knowledge far advanced to what we know? Why was this particular mountain chosen? Did aliens land to repair their spacecraft, or was this a way station for extraterrestrial travellers? Most puzzling is why they have not returned in the last 200 years.

Giant of Holly Creek

In 1965 Kenneth White built several stalls for his cattle under a large, overhanging rock ledge near his home on Holly Creek in eastcentral Kentucky.

During the process of cleaning out an accumulation of leaves, dirt and debris under the cliff, he had found a perfectly preserved skeleton which he thought might prove to be an Indian. The position of the skeleton indicated the body had been buried facing east. He found nothing buried with the skeleton.

White asked me to examine it with him. All of the bones were well preserved, including the fingers and toes. As we reassembled the skeleton, my first reaction was curiosity, which soon turned to amazement. The assembled skeleton measured 8 feet, 9 inches in length. The arms were extremely long, and the hands were large. By comparison, the feet were very small. The skull raised even more questions. It measured 30 inches in circumference. The eye and nose sockets were slits rather than cavities, and the area where the jawbone hinges to the skull was solid bone. It would seem that the person could not have opened his mouth. I have never heard of another person or skeleton which fits such a description.

The bones were covered with a powdery white substance which disappeared when touched. No weapons, clothing remains or tools were found with the skeleton which had been buried at least five feet underground. According to archaeologists, this would indicate that it had been there for over 300 years.

We assumed the skeleton to be the remains of an extraordinarily large, deformed Indian. Our assumption was based on the discovery 20 years previously of a 60-pound, double-edged granite Indian war ax and a flint knife with a 20-inch blade which had been plowed up in the same area by a farmer named Terry. These relics were kept by the Terry family for a few years before being lost. White later reburied the bones, and to my knowledge, no scientific examination was ever made of them.

Several questions concerning this skeleton remain unanswered. If this person was buried with clothing, weapons or tools, what happened to them? What was the white powdery substance covering the bones? Did the substance keep the bones from decaying, and if so, why did it not protect the flesh from decomposition? Could the skeleton have been stripped of all body tissue before burial, such as the ancient Hawaiians are known to have done? There was no dark soil around the skeleton. This is normally present when a body decays and has been buried for several years. If I did not know it was impossible, I would swear, from the condition of the skeleton, that the body had been prepared for burial and placed under the cliff only a few days before my friend dug it up.

Author's Note: There are several other recorded instances of this same type of skeleton being found elsewhere in Kentucky, Pennsylvania, Wisconsin and Arizona. The skeleton in Pennsylvania had six-inch horns in its skull.

Journey of the Ring

Daniel Busk of Barwick, Kentucky, narrated this strange tale to me in 1958. Fondly called "Uncle Dan" at the age of 94, he could remember events 80 years past as if they had happened only a few days ago.

Josephine Tyler and George Thomas had been married only a few months in the spring of 1862 when George decided to join the Union Army. Leaving his young pregnant wife, he rode to Lexington, Kentucky, to enlist.

Young Josephine lived in a cabin near her father's property while her husband was away, and in due time, a baby son was born...a son never to be seen by his father.

Everyone thought the war would be over in a few months; but the months dragged into a year, and Josie began to worry about her husband. She had received only three letters from him, telling of places he had been and battles in which he had fought. In his final letter, still owned by one of his descendants, George told Josie that he loved her and would somehow see that she would get his wedding ring if he should be killed.

Several months passed with no further word from George, and Josie wrote the U.S. War Department. Imagine her surprise and anguish when they reported that George had been killed in action the previous year over 300 miles from home. Josie never actually knew who had written the last letter from George, but the handwriting was the same on all three.

On a particular July night in 1865, Josie was eating supper with her brother and young son when their six dogs started barking and fighting over something outside. Taking a lantern, Josie and her brother went to see the cause of this commotion and saw that the dogs were fighting over a man's hand. Josie's brother ran them off by yelling and shooting a gun.

When Josie reached to pick up the hand and put it out of the dog's reach, she noticed a long, red scar. Her heart skipped a beat. The scar looked exactly like one on the back of her husband's left hand. Looking closer in the light of the lantern, Josie saw a wedding band on the third finger. Although trembling with fear, she removed the ring from the hand. Inside the ring were the initials GT and JT. Josie screamed in anguish... this was the ring her husband had worn when he rode off to war. Putting the hand between two boards in the fence, Josie and her brother took the ring inside the house.

The next morning, when they looked for the hand, it was gone.

Author's Note: How could a man's hand possibly stay preserved for two years after death? Where had the hand been since George's death? How did it find its way home? Who wrote the third letter saying that Josie would get her husband's ring no matter what happened to him?

Living Vision of John Lewis

The Reverend John H. Lewis

The Reverend John H. Lewis lived with his family in Perryville, Kentucky. He developed a throat ailment in the spring of 1938 which left him unable to preach for several weeks. On one of his weekly visits to his doctor in Lexington, Kentucky, his car suddenly stopped for no apparent reason.

As Lewis sat there pondering his problems in light of the fact that the car had just been recently serviced, the windshield began to fog, and a map of eastern Kentucky appeared with Breathitt County in the center. An inner voice seemed to tell him that he was needed for something important in that area of Kentucky. The foggy map remained until Lewis agreed to answer this call. When he did, the car started immediately, and his throat ailment also disappeared.

At the annual conference of ministers the following September, the Reverend Lewis was advised that a church in Jackson, county seat of Breathitt County, was open. He requested that he be given the pastorate. He had originally planned to go into the foreign mission field upon entering the ministry, but had been unable to do so because of illness. Now he was convinced that he was to serve his church within Kentucky rather than a foreign land.

After several years in Jackson, Reverend Lewis talked to church officials about opening a mission store in Breathitt County. He told them about his vision of several years before. Even though it was the enlightened days of the early 1940s, these men knew the Reverend Lewis was an honest, dependable person and did not ridicule or question what he told them. They decided to cooperate in the proposed endeavor.

A building was rented, and arrangements were made with other churches throughout Kentucky to furnish clothing, furniture and tools, which could be repaired and then sold at low prices in a store located at Jackson. Not only did they sell to the needy families in the area, but needy persons were employed by the store. Monies received through sales went to help the poor.

This undertaking became a very successful, continuing enterprise. The one store in Jackson soon expanded to five in eastern Kentucky with 50 to 75 people directly employed in different stores. This chain of stores Lewis helped to establish stands as a testimony to the work of this dedicated man. Today, they are known as the Methodist Mountain Mission Stores and have been helpful to countless persons.

This family story has been related to me numerous times,

and being the son-in-law of the Reverend Lewis, I was given permission to write about his experience.

John H. Lewis died in 1965, a highly respected man in his community and state. He lived to see what was, without question, a God-inspired vision come true.

"Suffer Not a Witch..."

In October 1976, a newspaper reporter in northcentral Kentucky wrote a story about the only known execution of a witch in Kentucky. He knew the year of the execution— 1823—but had been unable to determine where the witch's remains were buried. The article asked for any information that would help locate her grave site. At that time, I had never heard the woman's name, and knew nothing of how or when she died.

Later I was hiking with four other men along a ridge above the Ohio River...the same area the reporter had written about. We came upon the foundations of an old house which was almost hidden in the timber. While the others walked on, I decided to check the remains of this old house. Scattered everywhere was the usual debris of an abandoned country home. It was a quiet, lonely place. Only the far-off barking of a dog, the song of a meadowlark, the wind broke the silence. Later I learned that no one had lived on this old farm for the past 60 or 70 years.

Standing there alone, I noticed the faint outline of what had once been a lane. It led down a small hill where its identity was completely lost in the woods. Knowing the other men would wait farther on, I decided to follow this long-forgotten trail to see where it might lead.

After walking down the hill several hundred yards, my attention was drawn to a clump of wild rose bushes a short distance from the path. It seemed strangely out of place in the woods since wild roses normally grow in open fields. Pushing my way through the thicket, I suddenly came upon a rough gravestone almost covered with leaves and soil. It appeared to be lying at the end of a slight depression in the

Grave marker of Elizabeth Tincheor. I deliberately photographed the gravestone so that the name cannot be seen.

ground, a depression normally associated with an old grave after it sinks. The gravestone's appearance indicated that it had weathered many seasons.

After cleaning away the debris, the inscription was visible. Written in beautiful script was "Elizabeth Tincheor, 1799-1823." Directly beneath the name and dates had also been carved the words, "Suffer not a witch to live." No roots of the rose bushes appeared to have grown under or around the headstone. The flowers seemed to bend over in an attempt to conceal the marker from prying eyes. After taking a photograph, I replaced the marker. Then I pushed the rose bushes back together so that no one passing would see the stone or know anyone had been there. There is no explanation on how or why I found it, although I do recall that it was one of the most beautiful autumn days I had ever seen—October 17, 1976.

Upon returning home, I recalled the newspaper story about a witch being executed in that area. Calling the reporter, I asked him about the supposed witch...her name, the year of her execution and her age at the time. He replied. "Elizabeth Tincheor, October 17, 1823, and she was 24 years old." Somehow his answer wasn't a surprise. The reporter was anxious to learn the location of the grave and headstone so he could do a follow-up story, including photographs. But I could not bring myself to tell him where it was. I had the feeling that, while she lived, Elizabeth Tincheor saw too much of life's bitterness and too little of its kindness. Her secret resting place is safe.

Author's Note: I found Elizabeth Tincheor's grave site exactly 153 years, to the day, after she was executed. I am told by persons who have expertise in the study of numerology that 153 is a lucky number for those who experience it.

"I Curse the Ground"

It was the early 1920s, and Larry Malone, like many other young men, craved excitement. This led him to seek out the rougher elements in the rougher areas of the large south-central Kentucky town where he lived with his widowed mother.

After several escapades involving the police, Larry became known as a troublemaker. As he grew older, his boyish pranks turned to more serious crimes. He graduated from petty thievery and weekend drinking sprees to running bootleg whiskey and other even more alarming crimes. He had not killed anyone but had been in several shootouts with police and local gangs. Finally, the local political machine decided to get rid of Larry and his boisterous friends.

Throughout this time, moving within the shadow of major crime, Larry still lived with and supported his widowed mother. Larry, at the age of 25, met a young woman who seemed to mean enough to him that he would consider giving up his life of crime. But as fate would have it, this was the time when the local gangs decided to frame Larry for murder.

One night after drinking more whiskey than usual, Larry took his girlfriend home about 11:00 p.m. Then he parked his car alongside the road several miles from where she lived, and slept for three hours. He had awakened and was on his way back to town when he saw a car overturned in the middle of the road with someone lying beside it. Stopping to investigate the accident, Larry was suddenly surrounded by three men who came out of the darkness. One of the men knocked him unconscious with a blackjack. They then poured whiskey over him and forced some into his mouth. Placing a gun in Larry's hand, the men left the scene with

Larry's car. Using a disguised voice, one of the men telephoned the sheriff's office, telling him that they had passed a wrecked car on a road leading into town. The driver appeared to be hurt, and Larry Malone was sitting beside the car.

When the sheriff and two deputies arrived at the scene, they found Larry sitting beside the wreck with a gun in his hand. It proved to be the one used to kill the driver of the car. The dead man was a local gangster named "Chip" Carter, whom Larry had sworn to kill. The overturned car was the only car at the scene. Larry's car, taken by the three unknown men, was never seen again. The lump on Larry's head was presumed to to have been caused when the car turned over. Also, Larry was holding the murder weapon and had no alibi for the last three hours. There was only one conclusion that could be made, since the evidence against Larry was so overwhelming.

As there were no witnesses to testify, the only possible verdict at Larry Malone's trial for first-degree murder was "Guilty." He was sentenced to die in the electric chair.

A few days before his sentence was carried out, Larry's mother committed suicide. Just before he died, Larry made this statement: "I have done a lot of wrong things in my life, but I am innocent of killing Chip Carter. No matter where you bury me, nothing will ever grow on my grave. I curse the ground you put me in."

Everyone ignored this prediction until two years later when the caretaker of the cemetery where Larry Malone was buried noticed that no vegetation was growing on his grave. During the last 50 years, attempts have been made to get some type of vegetation to grow on his grave. The skeptics and agriculturists have tried every method they can devise to grow trees, or even weeds, on this spot, but without success. Everything that has been planted sprouts for a short time, withers and dies.

"Big Foot" in Kentucky

It was along this timberline that a "Bigfoot" was seen by the Fredericks family in 1979.

Sightings of Big Foot are usually reported in the western United States. But stories have been told through the years by people who claim to have encountered one of the creatures in Kentucky.

My father and one of my uncles were hunting squirrels in southern Perry County, Kentucky, in 1910. As they walked along a high ridge, they suddenly heard the sounds of a ferocious fight between their dog and some kind of animal. The dog, which had been out of sight around a cliff, yelped in pain. They rounded the cliff edge and saw a huge, brown, man-like creature that walked upright. The creature had broken the dog's spine in several places. As the creature turned, my uncle shot it at point-blank range with a 12-gauge shotgun loaded with buckshot. It didn't appear to feel anything. It jumped off the cliff edge, which was at least 15 feet straight down, and ran into the timber. Afterwards, several other people reported seeing the animal in that same area. These are among the earliest known sightings in Kentucky.

In the fall of 1935, James Collins, Dale Carpenter and Wilgus Prater ran a trap-line in the rugged section of Quicksand Creek in eastern Breathitt County, Kentucky. Game was plentiful that year, but, each time an animal was caught in a trap, it somehow escaped. After several days, the men decided they would try and capture whatever had been stealing the catches from their traps.

That night the men stationed themselves about a hundred yards apart under the ledge of a long, sloping rock overhang where the largest number of catches had been lost. They agreed to signal with a single rifle shot if anything unusual was seen. At the sound of the shot, they would converge and capture or kill whatever predator had been stealing their catches.

About 1:00 a.m. on the third night, Prater saw by moonlight, a large, hairy, brute-like animal walking upright and coming quietly toward the trap-line. Prater pumped three shots from a 30-30 rifle into the creature when it was within 20 feet of him. At the sound of gunfire, Carpenter and Collins hurriedly joined Prater. They could hear the creature growling and thrashing around in the brush, and following the sounds, the men slipped within a few yards of the animal and fired over 20 rounds in its direction. All was quiet as the echoes of the gunshots died. After deciding to wait for daylight to investigate, the men spent the rest of the night huddled under the cliff. The next morning, when they looked for the animal, they could find nothing. There were no tracks, no blood stains, no broken shrubbery, nothing to indicate the creature had been there. These men were honest, sober woodsmen who did not relate their experience until much later. All three were expert shots and swore until they died that they had fired over 20 rounds at a huge, hairy animal at a distance of less than five yards without killing or, apparently, even hitting it.

In 1979, William Fredericks and his family, along with several others, were picnicking in a park on the bank of the Ohio River in western Kentucky. As the men were pitching horseshoes, the children came running from the woods screaming that a large, black, hairy ape was chasing them. Going to investigate, the men reached the timberline and saw what appeared to be an ape over seven feet tall.

Frederick's brother-in-law fired six times at the creature from a distance of about 10 feet with a .45-caliber automatic pistol. The shots did not seem to affect the animal, which turned and ran down the riverbank. The men followed at a safe distance and saw several footprints in the mud. They measured 15½ inches long and 6 inches wide.

Near Maysville, Kentucky, in 1980, Dennis Patterson, his wife, mother-in-law and one daughter were watching television in his mobile home when another small daughter who had been asleep came into the living room and asked what was the big gray thing looking in her bedroom window. Patterson grabbed a .22-automatic pistol and a flashlight and started to go outside to investigate. But the creature had walked around the mobile home and was standing in front of the door when Patterson opened it. He flashed the light in the creature's eyes and, at the same time, emptied the gun into its chest. Patterson said that the top of his head came to the creature's shoulders...and Patterson is six feet tall. The animal appeared to be afraid of the light, but the pistol shots didn't seem to affect it.

A few days after this incident, a creature answering the same description went onto the screened-in back porch of Patterson's neighbor. It broke the lid off a 22-cubic-foot freezer and took all the frozen meat it could carry. Patterson's neighbor said that when he heard noise on the back porch, he went to investigate and saw a huge, hairy, gray-colored animal running upright towards the woods in back of his home. These two incidents were the only ones in which the creature was described as gray...most sightings indicated that the animal was black or brown.

I interviewed all the people mentioned and visited the places where these sightings took place. There is no attempt to explain this phenomenon, but I do think the persons involved believe what they saw. Several of the different Indian tribes have oral traditions of a man-like creature that has been seen all over the United States for the last 2,000 years.

Kentucky Methuselah: George Madison Henry

When the earliest settlers began to build cabins and take up land grants in eastern Kentucky during the late 1700s and early 1800s, they found a Negro man already living on the Middle Fork of the Kentucky River. He said his name was George Madison Henry and that he had moved from the tide-water country of Virginia to eastern Kentucky in 1790.

Henry seemed to have plenty of money for supplies and spent his time trapping and fishing. He did go on trips that would last from a week to a month, but no one ever knew where he went or what he did. For the first 30 or 40 years, as the area was filling up with people, no one noticed that Henry seemed not to age. Although he seemed to prefer the solitude of the woods, Henry was jovial and made friends with all his neighbors. He was always on hand to help anyone in trouble.

Years passed and several people made lasting friendships with Henry. When he was in a conversation with a neighbor sometimes Henry would refer to the General, James, Patrick, and Tom. When someone asked him who these men were, Henry replied, "Why, General Washington, Mr. James Madison, Patrick Henry and Tom Jefferson. I knowed them all." The neighbor thought that Henry had spent too much time alone in the woods and was fantasizing or was just plain crazy.

Henry made a trip to Washington, D.C., in 1836. When he returned home, he told his neighbors that he had attended the funeral of Mr. James Madison, the last of the men he had served. This information raised the eyebrows of

Henry's acquaintances.

After two generations, the older settlers began to die. The younger ones began to wonder about Henry. He looked the same to them as he had to their grandparents, but no one questioned him about his age. In 1900, Henry opened a small general store frequented by old-timers in the area. One of the aged white men, having known Henry for over 70 years, finally asked him how old he was.

Henry answered, "I wuz born August 15, 1755, on a plantation in Virginia. I wuz a body servant to General Washington during the war with England. I served Mr. Jefferson and Mr. Madison. I knowed Mr. Patrick Henry and a lot of them other folks what wuz in thet war. I even took care of Mr. Lafayette's hoss one time. He gave me a brace of his pistols."

The old-timers did not question Henry's integrity since some had heard great-grandparents say they knew Henry, and that was over 100 years before.

Henry continued to live and operate his store until 1930 when he was found dead in his small house behind the store. An investigation was made by the sheriff's department and a doctor. They stated in their report that Henry had apparently grown tired of living and had just gone to sleep.

A locked leather trunk was found in a closet of the house. None of the local folks had ever seen it. When it was opened the officers were dumbfounded to find letters from Washington, Madison, Patrick Henry and Thomas Jefferson. There were also antique pistols inscribed "To George Madison Henry from George Washington," a letter freeing Henry from slavery dated October 20, 1782, from Thomas Jefferson, and a book autographed by Jefferson.

Another letter, dated October 27, 1772, had been written by Judge Elias Adams and stated that Henry had been given a tract of land in the western country. At that time, it was Fincastle County, Virginia, and later became Kentucky. There was a well-worn Bible with Henry's birth date, August 15, 1755, written in it, a pair of expensive cuff links, a ring, several bills of Continental currency, English coins and another pair of pistols inscribed "Marquis de Lafayette." A suit of clothes from the period 1750-1800 was found. It included a ruffled shirt, long coat, wig, gold snuff box and silver-buckled shoes. All the items had been packed neatly in the leather trunk, and since Henry had no relatives, these antiques were sent to a museum in Washington, D.C.

My grandfather had spoken about George Henry, saying that Henry claimed to have been in the Revolutionary War. Nobody had believed him since he didn't look to be over 50 years old when he died, but my grandfather had known Henry for over 60 years.

Several people still living can remember when Henry died, and occasionally the story of Henry's longevity is mentioned by old-timers in the area. Incredibly, the evidence points to the fact that the man named George Madison Henry served in the Revolutionary War as a slave, earned the respect of its leaders and was given his freedom by Thomas Jefferson. This man then lived until 1930, which made him 175 years old.

Willard Craft's Incredible Journey

Teleportation, the instantaneous transportation of a human being from one place to another, is said to be usually accompanied by a flash of light. It leaves the subject in a state of shock with no memory of what has happened. Although it seems incredible that a living person can be disintegrated in one spot and materialized in another, a number of such cases have reportedly been verified.

The best known instance of human teleportation is that of Elijah, recorded in the Bible (II Kings 2:11, 16-18). He was taken skyward in a blaze of light and a whirlwind. The incident was witnessed by the prophet Elisha, who said that God had taken Elijah to heaven in a chariot of fire! Fifty men searched for three days on the mountain where Elijah disappeared, but no trace of his body was ever found.

A more current instance involved a man from eastcentral Kentucky. On a snowy day in January 1886, Willard Craft was walking to church. He was late for the service, and, since he had the best voice in the choir, eight church members had stepped outside to see if he was coming along the road. They did see Craft walking in the snow about 200 yards from the church. Suddenly, there was a blinding flash of light, and Willard Craft disappeared! The church people rushed to where Craft had been walking. His tracks, leading into a wide circle where the snow had been melted by some intense heat, were all they found.

This was coal mining country, where occasionally pockets of natural gas has been found over the years. Some thought that one of these might have exploded and blown Craft into the nearby timber. An intensive search of the surrounding area was made, but no sign of a body was found.

Craft had been a sober, hard-working young man, supporting his widowed mother, and was sadly missed in the community. Several months later, the townspeople decided to erect a stone in the local cemetery to the memory of Willard Craft, although his body had not been found. The marker gave his name, date of birth and death; it also stated, "Died from Causes Unknown."

Most folks eventually forgot about Craft's disappearance. About four years later, a letter arrived at the small post office addressed to Willard Craft's mother. It was from her son. In the letter Craft explained that he had been living in Canada for four years without knowing who he was or where he came from. He had been in a sawmill explosion while working in the log woods; and following an operation to remove pieces of metal from his head, he had suddenly regained his memory. The letter was written from a hospital in Edmonton, Canada.

Several weeks later, after his recuperation, Willard Craft returned home, and the entire community turned out to see the arrival of the man they all had thought was dead. Craft had not changed; neither did he have an explanation for what had happened—all he recalled was the bright flash of light in which he had disappeared. He had no idea how he had gotten nearly 2,500 miles from his home in Kentucky to western Canada or what he had been doing during the four years of his amnesia. It seemed logical, however, that Craft had obtained a job in the log woods since he was experienced in that type of work.

The melted circle in the snow and the flash of light seen by the eyewitnesses were never explained, and Craft never did remember anything that happened to him during the four years of his disappearance.

Since this strange incident agrees with the descriptions of several other documented cases of human teleportation, it would seem the only answer to William Craft's disappearance and loss of memory is that he, through some auspices, had been teleported to Canada. There was enough validity in this case for it to be considered for publication several years ago in Robert Ripley's *Believe It Or Not*.

The Vengeful Witch

In the early 1900s, an old lady known only as the "Widow Simpson" lived in a cabin near the head of Lick Branch, a tributary to the North Fork of the Kentucky River in south-eastern Kentucky. No one knew her age, and no one ever knew where she came from or how long she had lived in the cabin with her cats and assorted other animals. People considered her a witch, not only because of her strange behavior, but because of the odd and unusual incidents that occurred in the neighborhood. She seemed to know if someone had spoken ill of her, and she vehemently protested if anyone trespassed on her property. Anyone guilty of either offense always had something bad happen to them.

A farmer to who had crossed the Widow Simpson's property without permission began to notice strange happenings around his farm. One morning his sheep were in the pen with his hogs, yet the gate to the sheep pen was securely locked. Later that day, he could not chase away a large cow that followed him while he plowed. The cow followed him until he went home. On the very next day, his team of mules were spooked by something he could not see. They ran away and destroyed a brand new wagon. On still another day, a crow flew down, snatched his hat, then flew away. He found the hat later hanging on a fence post near the barn. The farmer also suffered a bite by a strange dog and was chased by a wildcat. Two of his cows began to give bloody milk, and several died. The farmer was convinced that he should visit the widow and apologize. He did, and the unusual happenings stopped.

One local housewife made the mistake of telling a neighbor that she thought the Widow Simpson was the ugliest woman in the county. When she went into her bedroom the next night, objects were tossed about the room, a window was broken and clothes were on the floor. She straightened the disarray; but, again on the next night, the bed clothing was thrown on the floor, the furniture was turned over, and mirrors were broken. When she started into the room, she heard a woman's hysterical laughter. The woman was unnerved almost to the point of insanity. Her husband suggested that she apologize to the Widow Simpson for her remarks, and, when this was done, the strange incidents stopped.

A young man, who went squirrel hunting on the widow's property without her permission, noticed a part of his rifle was missing when he returned home. He thought he had lost it in the woods and did not worry about it.

That night his sleep was interrupted by nightmares which left him exhausted by morning. During the nights that followed he found little rest. Once he was awakened by something cold pressed against his face. When he lit a lamp, he saw a large black dog—which immediately vanished.

He awoke one morning feeling unusually tired; then he remembered dreaming that the Widow Simpson had turned him into a horse, which she rode all night. He looked at his hands and feet and found them covered with mud and badly scratched, as if he had been running through briars.

After several nights of this torture, the youth moved far away from the community.

No one could prove the widow had anything to do with any of these incidents. After all, she had never visited any of the people involved. Things might have continued in this manner had it not been for a circumstance which, at first, did not seem to involve the widow.

Ten men, hunting with 20 fox hounds, were on a ridge several miles from the widow's property. During the hunt they saw a fox that seemed to glow in the dark. They had never seen such an animal before. Men and dogs chased the strange fox for miles, and in the darkness, went onto the widow's property without realizing it. They continued the chase throughout the night until the fox finally led them to the

Widow Simpson's, where the animal seemed to disappear through the cabin wall.

The extremely angry widow came out of the house to meet the men. One man later described the early morning confrontation: "The widow was madder than hell! The dogs were barking with some of us trying to hold them, and we were out of breath. We all knew there would be trouble since we had chased what we now believed to be one of the widow's pets and were on her property. She looked at us and said, 'Your guns will never hit anything again when you hunt, and all of you, with your dogs, will soon die. Get off my land and don't come back.' We all left in a hurry."

In the days that followed, all the men who had pursued the glowing fox noticed that they could not hit anything when they shot their rifles. Their dogs began to die one by one, but no one became particularly alarmed until two of the men were killed in freak accidents. Shortly thereafter, three more became sick and died for no apparent reason.

Two of the remaining five hunters moved out of the neighborhood and never returned to the area; and it is not known if anything unusual happened to them. The final three began to wonder what would happen to them...within days, two of these men were found dead, their bodies leaning against a tree. There was a look of horror on each face, as if they had died looking at something ghastly. No one ever determined what they saw or how they died, since both were in good health and neither had any wounds. There was also speculation about why the bodies remained standing after death— they looked like they had been turned to stone.

Orvil Adams, the last of 10 hunters still in the area, was determined that no witch was going to cause his death. When he heard of Mort Jeffries, living in the next county, who could break a witch's spell, Orvil went to him and told Jeffries the whole story. Jeffries advised Orvil to get a silver dollar, a piece of gum resin from a pine tree, and two hairs from the tail of a fox, and then come back in exactly one week.

Orvil returned at the appointed time. Jeffries took him to a place where he had set up small wooden sticks to make an outline shaped like a fox. "The witch takes the shape of a fox, and the only way to kill her and break the spell is to do exactly what I tell you. If you don't do this, you are a dead man."

Orvil was ready to do anything Jeffries said in order to break the witch's hold and to save his life. Jeffries melted the silver dollar and made it into a bullet cartridge to fit Orvil's rifle. The two fox hairs were crossed and stuck to the rifle's front sight with the gum resin. Jeffries told Orvil to measure 13 yards exactly from the outline of the fox, check the time by his watch, then fire his rifle into the target. Orvil did as instructed.

Later he said that when the bullet hit the target, he felt as if he were on fire for a few seconds; then he felt normal again.

Upon returning home, Orvil learned that the widow had been found dead—she died at the exact moment Orvil hit the target of the fox with the silver bullet. According to the doctor who examined her, there were no marks on her body.

To assure that no more incidents connected with the Widow Simpson could occur, she was buried in an unmarked grave; then her cabin and everything in it was burned. No other incidents of witchcraft were ever reported in the neighborhood again.

Dancing Smoke

Old churches, with their accompanying cemeteries, are fertile ground for ghost stories and unexplained phenomena.

During the 1930s, a major highway being built in east-central Kentucky was routed directly through a country graveyard. The construction company reached an agreement with those who had relatives buried there to move all the bodies to a new location.

Wayne Morgan, foreman of the work crew, and Charles Lawton, a crew member, made an initial examination of the graves in preparation for moving the bodies before the heavy road-building equipment reached the site. They were nearly through by about 4:00 p.m. when they saw something totally uncanny. Two round balls of what appeared to be dense smoke were bobbing up and down in a neglected, weed-choked corner of the graveyard.

The men found the caretaker, and Morgan told him about the strange spheres. Baffled, the caretaker went with the workmen to the vacant corner where the strange balls continued to bounce about in the air. When the three walked closer, the circles disappeared.

Though Morgan, Lawton and the caretaker checked the ground carefully, they found no overlooked grave markers or anything out of the ordinary. None of the three believed in ghosts, but they realized they had seen something mysterious and could not explain it.

When the crew came to work the next morning, they were surprised to find a space the size of a small grave had been cleared in the previously overgrown corner. Two vases of fresh wildflowers had been set in the center of the plot.

At about 10:00 a.m. the balls of smoke reappeared, witnessed this time by the entire 12-man crew. In the weeks that followed, the workers continued moving the bodies to the new location and tried to ignore the two spheres that persistently appeared every day.

One morning, when most of the graves had been relocated, the crewmen arrived at the cemetery and were stunned to find their work tools stacked on the spot where the flower vases had been. Even more astounding was that the tools had been locked in a tool box the night before, and the lock was still in place! This latest unexplainable circumstance unnerved the crew to the point that some were ready to quit. There were only four more bodies to move, though, and they could be done in a few hours—the men voted to complete the job.

The bobbing circular clouds of smoke were present as usual while the final graves were moved. As the last one was cleared away, the balls became extremely agitated, bobbing and turning, approaching the crew members and then returning to the cleared plot in the corner. Morgan watched the erratic, dancing smoke and finally said to the men, "I don't know what those bobbing things mean, but we are going to dig up that plot and see what is in it."

When they had dug about three feet down, they found a flat rock—its surface was roughly three feet square. Beneath the slab, in a stone-lined, coffin-shaped depression, lay the skeletons of two young children. The crew gently placed the small skeletons in a wooden coffin and carefully removed it to the new burial site.

And the fluttering smoke vanished.

No one ever learned the identity of the two children or when they had been buried. An elderly man in the neighborhood remembered gypsies camping near the cemetery some 50 years before. Perhaps it was one of these nomadic families who had buried the children.

One thing is known, however...after the cemetery was cleared of **all** bodies, the bobbing spheres of smoke were never seen again.

It was in a cemetery such as this (before the bodies were removed) that the two balls of smokey light were seen by a work crew.

Places of Silence

There are two spots in Kentucky where radios, walkie-talkies, or any other things electronic will not work. One is in eastcentral Kentucky, and the other is in the northcentral area. Different brands and models of radios and CBs have been tried—car, transistor and battery powered—but, past an invisible line, they all stop working.

The place in eastcentral Kentucky is at the mouth of a large stream. Start up this creek with any radio, and it stops instantly until one travels about 25 steps; then it starts again. The same strange thing occurs at the other location.

Engineers, psychics and geologists have been contacted and questioned about this unusual occurrence, but they have no explanation. Suggestions have been made that this phenomenon is caused by a magnetic field, by low elevation or by nearness to water, but no satisfactory or logical answer has ever been found.

This phenomenon apparently occurs only in Kentucky, since my research did not turn up any other place in the world where it happens. It is just another of the strange, unexplained happenings within the state encountered in my search for the unusual.

AFTERWORD

There can be no epilogue to this collection of Kentucky folklore...stories and events are timeless. Man has always had his myths, legends, stories, dreams and unexplained phenomena of nature and himself. They are part of his heritage, without which he could not exist.